BEGONIAS, GLOXINIAS AND
AFRICAN VIOLETS

H. G. WITHAM FOGG

Begonias, Gloxinias
and
African Violets

GARDEN BOOK CLUB
121 CHARING CROSS ROAD
LONDON, W.C.2

Printed in Great Britain
by Bristol Typesetting Co. Ltd.,
Barton Manor, St. Philips, Bristol 2

Contents

CHAPTER ONE

The Development of the Begonia

THE BEGONIA as we know it today, is very different from the plant which was first discovered by the botanist Plumier. History is valuable in not only giving the origin of a plant but in revealing the conditions of its natural environment. It is a fact, that many plants which have been cultivated in this country for many years, still have underlying needs such as are satisfied in their natural habitat, which one should endeavour to fulfil as far as possible.

A knowledge of the background of the begonia, does give a better understanding of its characteristics, habit, and limitations. With this knowledge, we are able to provide as far as possible, conditions likely to suit the plant, and also to give just that little extra attention which makes all the difference between real success and indifferent results.

The begonia family is a large one. It is estimated that the species alone number many hundreds, while the number of hybrids must run into many thousands. The bulk of these, of course, are little known. These plants fall into three main groups, the tuberous rooted, the rhizomatous, and the fibrous rooted. Then of course, there are a number of divisions in each of these groups, and it is sometimes difficult to place some of the hybrids in a particular group.

One great advantage in growing various members of the begonia family, is that by using some of the tuberous rooted and some of the foliage sorts, it is possible to have an ornamental display throughout the year.

Obviously we can only mention a comparatively few of the species and varieties and must concentrate on those which are available and are most likely to be of value to the average gardener and begonia lover in particular, although it is hoped that with further knowledge of the begonia family, many other gardeners will fall under the spell of this most attractive plant.

In dealing with events concerning the discovery and development of the begonia, which took place several hundred years ago, it is not difficult for some of the details to become a little clouded or out of order. This is especially so since some species of the plant we now know as the begonia, were originally cultivated under different names, when they were first found in Mexico. As with other families of plants it is fortunate that there were and still are, individuals and firms prepared to spare time and effort to increase the knowledge of the family and to hunt abroad for a new species and to introduce new varieties through skilful hybridising.

Beginning with details of history for which there is sound grounds of belief, we find that Plumier, the early botanist and monk, who showed such interest in many other plants, is credited with the discovery of the begonia, towards the end of the seventeenth century.

The plant he found could not be placed in any known genus, and Plumier, as had been done with other discoveries which he had named after someone whom he admired, decided to bring into being a new genus. This was named after Michel Begon a French botanist, who was also governor of Santo Domingo. Thus the name ' Begonia ' came into being.

It was not until the eighteenth century was well advanced, that the begonia was first seen in Britain, a plant having arrived at Kew Gardens. Subsequently, others came from both the West and East Indies.

Real interest and advance in knowledge, of the begonia however, did not begin until early in the nineteenth century and by the time another forty years had been reached, many species were known including some which we still hold dear, such as B. evansiana, maculata and gracilis.

Britain was not the only country interested, for work on hybridising had been carried out in several countries including the United States of America.

It was the discovery, apparently accidentally, of Begonia rex in a box of other plants, just over a hundred years ago, which raised the genus to a higher level in the eyes of horticulturally-minded people. From this time, it was not only the better-off people who were able to travel, who became concerned with the advancement of the begonia, but the average gardener as well.

Mexico, and the Indies have played a part in the history of this lovely plant; it is also true that Peru, Bolivia and other parts of South America have many wild species, while there are some in Africa and the Himalayas.

It appears that the first real shipment of the tuberous varieties took place in 1847. They were sent from Bolivia to the firm of Henderson. Then another shipment from the same country, came into the hands of Mr. James Veitch, a member of that once renowned firm of plant growers and distributors. He exhibited the plants at flower shows both in London and Paris, where they attracted great attention. It is believed that the begonia in question was B. boliviensis, which has bright red flowers.

Various crosses were made between this species and others, resulting in some good hybrids. One which can still be found in specialised collections is B. sedeni, which is named after John Seden, who was employed by Messrs. Veitch, and who made a number of successful crosses. B. sedeni, is the result of the crossing of B. boliviensis, and an undisclosed Andean species. This first cross was not only important in itself, but more so, because it became the basis on which many modern hybrids have been created.

Other early species which were much used in hybridising and of which some of the characteristics of the tuberous begonia of today may be seen, include B. pearcei and B. veitchii. These were brought into prominence by Richard Pearce who travelled widely for the firm of James Veitch of Chelsea. The latter species when in its native habitat, grows in partially shaded, fairly moist, woodland glades and high altitudes, and the fact that both pearcei and veitchii were largely used in hybridising, gives an indication as to why tuberous begonias can be grown so successfully under extremely different conditions. We may assume that most of the yellow and near yellow present day tuberous hybrids, have their origin in B. pearcei, while the stocky growth and large flowers of our best sorts, have come through B. veitchii.

Another Veitch development was B. rosaeflora, which has also been much used for hybridising, while B. davisii was introduced from Peru, and has given much to the basic qualities of good present day forms. All this time breeders in other countries were also working on the begonia, with a measure of success and fresh species were being found in South America. One, B. baumannii was introduced by Lemoine, the famous French breeder. This came from Bolivia and was actually sent by Lemoine to a German plant specialist named Baumanni, from whom the name was taken. One important feature of B. baumannii was its large size and its attractive scent. It is unfortunate that fragrance has not proved to be a dominant quality, although there are a few hybrids in cultivation which have perfume, and it seems likely that these originally came from crosses based on baumannii.

The first tuberous begonias available were single flowered sorts. Subsequently the famous French firm of Lemoine offered semi-double hybrids. In addition, the same firm produced plants having flowers with even more petals. Although the first batches of plants distributed were of little use, because they were of poor constitution, it eventually proved possible to distribute a first-class double tuberous begonia. This had as one of its parents, B. boliviensis, and it was named Glory of Nancy.

A considerable amount of valuable hybridising was also done by Crousse, another Frenchman, whose name is commemorated in various ways in the horticultural world. By the time the new hybrids were distributed, another important development had occurred in that the pendula or basket type of begonia was available in France and elsewhere.

At first, this was known as Begonia chrysanthemiflora

being later named B. tuberhybrida pendula flore plena. Various other firms both in this country and abroad, did valuable work in improving the begonia. Conspicuous among these was Messrs. Blackmore and Langdon of Bath, Somerset. This firm has continued with great success, to improve begonias and anyone who has seen the exhibits staged at the Chelsea Flower Show or other exhibitions will know how high is the standard reached.

The introduction of the all double tuberous begonia was followed by the production of hybrids in a wide colour range. Today, breeders in this country, the United States, and elsewhere abroad, have been able to secure flowers in almost all the basic colours. Other developments followed the coming of the hanging basket begonias and the bedding and Winter flowering types have now become very popular.

Although we now have begonias of very large size, there are still many double and single varieties which produce blooms of medium size. These look well when seen in the greenhouse, living-room and conservatory and also in window-boxes and hanging baskets and when bedded out of doors during the Summer. Then, of course, we must not overlook the many more wonderful species and varieties which have most ornamental foliage in many colour tones and shapes.

Here then we have in the begonia, a plant native of distant countries which has by the skilful patient work of plant breeders in this, and other continents been so improved that it rarely fails to do well. Almost everyone who sees well grown begonias, cannot fail to be thrilled and cheered by the display.

Apart from the more usual double begonias there are several other types or forms having attractively shaped or marked flowers. These include those with ruffled or rose-shaped flowers, both of which were originated by the firm of Vetterle and Reinelt of Capitola, California. The colour range in these takes in white, blush-pink, salmon-pink, carmine-rose, red, scarlet, yellow, apricot, orange and flame.

The new ruffled begonias are much different from the

tuberous begonias handled by growers a hundred years ago. Those produced about four small flowers. Today, these new ruffled varieties have flowers two or three times the size of their ancestors. The petals are frilled and ruffled most attractively and although the flowers are large, the heads are held up well on strong stems. Then there is the strain known as the carnation or Begonia fimbriata plena, with double frills. One of the most attractive introductions during recent years has been the new ruffled picotee type. After many years intensive breeding tubers have now become available in several good colours, and the flowers produced are most spectacular.

Yet another recent introduction is the Rose-form picotee, which may be regarded as a great advance in tuberous begonias. The plants produce well nigh perfect flowers and can be raised from seed in the usual way.

Although the present day begonias are so beautiful, we may be sure that the great skill of breeders in this country and abroad, will continue to be used to produce plants of even better constitution and having flowers with still greater beauty and, perhaps, it is not too much to hope, also with a good perfume.

However good the qualities of a plant and its flowers may be, if the blooms possess an attractive perfume, the value of the plant will be increased. Even if a flower is on the small side and it has perfume, it will usually attract as much or more attention, than a very large flower without scent.

With such an attractive subject as the begonia, the presence of fragrance would indeed be a great asset. We must not assume however, that this quality has been overlooked or ignored by hybridists, for it is between sixty or seventy years since the first scented tuberous begonia hybrids were produced.

They came from the species B. baumannii previously mentioned, and there appears to have been at one time, both single and double varieties which were fragrant. Various crosses were made and some success was achieved in producing a range of scented hybrids, although they do not now appear to be available, in this country, at least. The remarkable thing about many of these hybrids is that the perfume is chiefly noticeable during the early part of the day and seems to vanish at least temporarily, during the afternoons.

This is so in the case of a Scottish strain raised fifty years ago and of which the variety J. G. White is still sometimes available. This variety has medium-sized flowers, and in some respects seems to be half-way between the large-flowered and multiflora types. The cup-shaped, double blooms, are freely produced and the plant makes a really good bushy specimen when grown under ordinary conditions. A species, Begonia micranthera fimbriata was distributed in the U.S.A. thirty years ago, and from this a number of hybrids have been produced, some having attractive reddish stems with leaves lightly tinged pink. While the plant is a little ungainly in its habit, the blooms make up for this short-coming, since they are so delightfully scented, so much so, that one variety has been named Wild Rose.

Then several years ago, a number of pendula varieties were raised in the U.S.A. With the double, naturally drooping flowers of this type of begonia, combined with their delicate fragrance, they well deserve the name of Sweety, which has been given to the section.

As with other flowers, although it is known that perfume can be introduced, it is not easy to imagine how it can be achieved, although one may be sure that hybridists have endeavoured to do so and will continue their work in this connection. The process of introducing fragrance is bound to be a long and dull one, requiring patience and perseverance on the part of the hybridists, which fortunately from past achievements, we know is not lacking.

CHAPTER TWO

Starting the Tubers

THE GARDENER who wishes to commence growing begonias can begin by raising them from seed. which although inexpensive, is perhaps a little involved for the grower entirely inexperienced with these plants.

The easiest way to start is by purchasing tubers. which have already been grown from seed. Very large quantities of tubers are sold annually. They are available in separate named sorts as well as in mixtures. the advantage of growing tubers is that if named sorts are bought, one can be certain of the varieties and colours that are to be produced. Subsequently to produce any particular plant which is exactly the same as the parent, it must be done vegetatively as described later.

The dry or dormant tubers can be started into growth at any time from January until April. Unless very early blooms are required. it is best to wait until February. until then for the average greenhouse owner may find it difficult to sustain sufficient, even heat. Few of us will be able to provide enough warmth in the early part of the year in order to obtain blooms before July. Started in March and with very little heat, it is still possible to secure really first-class blooms from August onwards.

It is important to use firm. plump tubers. and any which are rather soft or show signs of decay are best discarded. If buying from a reliable firm, one can normally rely on the stock purchased. but where it has been necessary to store one's own tubers. and conditions have not been ideal a closer watch is necessary.

If the ripening and drying off process was not thorough the

previous autumn some tubers may show signs of rotting.

Ordinary seed trays are suitable for starting the tubers, or any shallow box of about three inches in depth will be convenient. At the bottom, place a layer of leaf mould or peat, then cover this with a good mixture made of one part each good loam, peat or leaf mould and a half a part of silver sand, or if it is possible use only peat. A lightish rooting medium is required, and one in which there is no possibility of waterlogging. The mixture should be nicely damp at planting time, but not sticky so that it cakes on being touched.

While it has long been the custom of amateur and professional growers to so place the tubers in the soil that the crowns are left uncovered, I notice from the handbook of the National Begonia Society that in a reported talk of Mr. S. C. Langdon of the famous begonia specialist firm of Blackmore and Langdon, it is advised that tubers should be pressed into the compost so that the crowns *are* covered. I was glad to read this, since I have long believed that the old theory of moisture settling on the indented crowns through their being covered, was incorrect. It is obvious that however carefully watering may be done, some spots of moisture are bound to settle on exposed tubers where they may very well cause trouble.

It has always been considered that the covering of the crowns is likely to lead to the setting in of decay because of the possibility of moisture settling on the flattish tubers. Mr. Langdon's well supported theory is that, with the tubers covered, the excess water is taken off the crowns by capillary action. It is certainly difficult when the tubers are not entirely buried, to prevent some moisture settling in the saucer-like top of the crowns. This, with the warm atmosphere of the greenhouse can easily provide conditions for rot to commence.

Another important advantage in covering the crowns is that it permits the full development of roots from the sides and even the top of the tuber. It will often be noticed that roots do commence to grow from the top but when this is left exposed, many of these fibrous roots shrivel to the detrement of the plant, although in a few cases, they do find an anchorage in the soil.

Although the tubers are usually started in pots, when a good number are involved and space is limited, they can be planted up in trays or boxes using the same soil mixture.

After planting, water the containers well, but do not make the compost a soggy mess. This should be the rule throughout. On the other hand, the soil must not dry out even for a short period. This is why it is an advantage to cover the trays or pots with paper until the first signs of growth are seen.

Provided the tubers are healthy in the first place, it is very unlikely that they will rot through being actually covered with soil. Another important point is to see that the tubers are planted the right way up – the hollow side should be uppermost.

I have never found it advisable to add any kind of fertiliser to the starting compost used. It is better for the plants that the roots should have to search for their feeding material, instead of finding it immediately around them, since the activity involved leads to stronger, healthier development. It is not necessary to use the John Innes composts, and unsterilised soil does give better results.

It is wisest to use the compost after it has been in the warm for a week or so, then it is more or less the same temperature as the greenhouse. Used straight from a frosty potting shed, the tubers will be longer in starting into growth. Even when different varieties are planted at the same time, it will be found that some are ready to pot up before others, and it is noticeable that the reds are usually before others, and even under identical conditions.

This of course, is why, when a tray of mixed tubers are planted, some will be much more forward than others. While the most forward tubers can be planted up before those starting later into growth, none should be disturbed until they have a good root system, and for this reason, the potting up may extend over a period. It is wise to look at the planted trays at frequent intervals so that should there be the slightest indication of rotting, the tubers concerned can be removed. Where it is only a small spot of decay the affected part can be cut away with a sharp knife. In such cases, the tubers are best replanted in a separate tray or pot, so that the possibility of the disease re-appearing and spreading is minimised.

During the early part of the year, when the tubers are being started into growth, the question of temperature in the greenhouse is often a real problem. As always, it is better to maintain a rather low temperature all the time, than to allow the thermometer to reach great heights during the day, and to fall sharply at night. For the amateur at least, an ideal even temperature would be 60 to 65 degrees F. but begonias will certainly be all right where only 55 degrees can be maintained. Lower than 50 degrees however, there is liable to be trouble with poor irregular growth, and a greater possibility of the tubers rotting.

At all times and especially when there is not a lot of heat, the use of very cold water should be avoided, and where tap water has to be used, this should be drawn off for some hours before use, so that the tubers do not suffer the shock of a cold bath. There is no need to apply much water before the tubers produce new growth. After that, more will be needed. If a propagating frame or any kind of bottom heat is available, so much the better, for such a provision will encourage a good root system before there is much top growth.

The aim should be to secure sturdy development and not weak, spindly shoots which will stand little chance of doing well. When potting the growing tubers take care not to break or damage the roots and where some tubers have to remain in the boxes, the holes left by the transferred growing tubers, should be filled with compost which will encourage the more backward ones to become active.

Do not over pot. The size of the first pot used will largely depend on the strength of the tuber. It is always best to start with a small pot and then to move the plants to larger receptacles as growth proceeds. The pots should be well crocked, or supplied with drainage material before putting in the soil mixture. Since begonia roots tend to spread outwards rather than to go down deeply, they will need a rather larger size pot than is the case with many other plants and it may be necessary to first use the four-inch size.

As growth proceeds, the plants will need moving to the five-inch pots, and with vigorous growers and where the object is to obtain specimen plants, more moves may be required according to the development made.

With the larger receptacles, extra feeding has to be provided to keep the plants in good condition. As far as the final potting is concerned, not only should the soil mixture be richer, but the compost must be made firmer.

Some liquid feeding can be given, but do not overdo it. In any case, it should not be commenced until the flower buds begin to show. Pinch out any flower buds which may appear before the plants are in their final pots and also if they show before the plants become established after the last move. In any event, these early buds are unlikely to produce worthwhile flowers. As previously stated, it is also permissible to remove the buds at a later stage with a view to timing the blooms. Experience is the best guide in this matter. This applies to the large flowered tuberous begonias and not to the smaller flowering pendula, multiflora or similar varieties.

The begonia pendula varieties which also have tuberous roots, are stated in exactly the same way as the double and single large flowered forms. The main difference is that after being moved on to the small pots, they are transferred direct to their flowering quarters in baskets or other receptacles, instead of being given several moves. They must not be placed outdoors until weather conditions are congenial, but the baskets can be hung up straight away in the greenhouse, or warm conservatory.

CHAPTER THREE

General Cultivation

T U B E R S   A R E usually started in trays of porous compost or peat and silver sand which should be nicely moist. Space them up to two inches apart and after planting give a light sprinkling of water. Cover the trays with paper and place them in the shade. The first potting should begin when the young plants have formed several leaves and are obviously growing well. It is a mistake to over pot, that is, to give very large pots until the plants are ready for them.

When transplanting, lift the tubers very carefully from the trays so that there is little or no damage to the roots. After a few weeks in the first pot it will be time for the second potting, which will normally be in the four or five-inch size. This will usually be sufficient for most tubers, although any particularly active plants with strong foliage, can be given a bigger size.

Many growers think that it is advisable to keep the plants slightly pot bound, believing in this way, they are likely to flower more freely. Much of course, will depend upon whether the plants are restricted to a single stem or if two or more are allowed.

Strong growers in big pots should be encouraged to make an easy root run, and this can be helped by using plenty of leaf mould in the compost, with of course, generous feeding. For the final potting the compost should be rather heavier, as well as richer and coarser. In addition, it must be made very firm.

Once the plants are really well rooted in their final pots and the flower buds begin to develop, liquid feeding can be started. This can be one of the proprietary brands or a liquid manure made up and used when it is the strength of weak tea. Over feeding of course, is harmful. Where really large flowers are required, it is often helpful to remove the first flower buds, although consideration must be given to timing if the flowers are needed for a special date.

Until the plants are really fully established, extra care is needed regarding watering, for soggy roots will soon decay. On the other hand, if the compost dries out for a short time, the flower buds may soon fall. Always make sure that the compost is moist before transferring the plants to larger pots which should be clean. It is when dirty pots are used that it is difficult to knock the plants out when required, and the roots suffer damage. It is only in the case of potting on old plants, that the soil needs shaking out, otherwise apart from removing the old crocks, there is no need to disturb the roots. Many growers find it better to use pans in preference to the deeper pots since the begonia roots do not go down deeply but are rather inclined to spread out.

Never allow water to settle on the leaves, and certainly not remain there at night. Should this happen it is liable to set up decay and fungus of various types may develop. It is advisable to water in the morning, particularly in cold or even dull weather Overhead sprayings are rarely required excepting during really hot, close weather, although even then, they should never be applied when the sun is shining directly on the foliage.

After the plants have been moved into the pots in which they are to flower, they must not be neglected. Attention must be given to watering, damping down, ventilation, supporting the plants and disbudding. Watering should always be done with care. At first, the plants will not need much moisture but once the root action becomes vigorous, and this will be seen by the strength of the top growth, water will be needed more frequently.

If the greenhouse is heated, the plants can be sprayed overhead with warm water. Do not do this however, when there is no heat, otherwise the foliage may become marked.

Ventilation is necessary whenever it is possible to give it without creating a draught.

Regarding staking, this is required as growth proceeds. Normally one inconspicuous stake for each plant is enough, unless of course, the specimen is a large one with more than one main stem.

For many growers the question of thinning and disbudding becomes a problem. Very often the plants produce more growths than are required for the development of a first-class plant. If therefore, the object is to obtain really large, well formed flowers, some of the growths must be removed.

The simplest method is to restrict one or two-year-old plants to one main stem with two good side shoots. This should result in well balanced plants which flower freely. The shoots or growths which are removed, can where required, be used as cuttings to increase stocks.

Disbudding simply means the removal of the female flowers. These are readily seen by the little seed pods they carry at the back of the flower and they are also produced on each side of the male blooms. It is, of course, only the male flowers which develop into large double blooms. Therefore, where really large blooms are required both for exhibition and general decoration, all the female flowers should be taken off as soon as they are big enough to handle.

The feeding of the large flowered begonias is also a problem to many gardeners. It is certainly helpful when really large blooms are required but there is no real secret in the procedure and quite inexperienced growers should have no difficulty in feeding the plants satisfactorily.

Perhaps the initial mistake that many growers make is to feed plants when they are weak and poor looking. This is a mistake, for feeding should not be done until the plants are strong and healthy, with a vigorous root action.

There are many suitable fertilisers now available and it is not now necessary to prepare liquid manures as was the case thirty or forty years ago. Several reliable firms make up their own proprietary brands of fertilisers. A well balanced soluble or liquid feed should be chosen, one which contains phosphates as well as nitrogen, etc.

Such fertilisers should be used once every fifteen to twenty days while the plants remain in flower. It is unwise to feed after the end of August, for from that time, the plants gradually begin to prepare for dormancy.

As we have indicated elsewhere, it is unwise to attempt to dry off begonias immediately they have finished flowering. The development and ripening of the tuber is controlled by the light factor and as the days shorten, from September onwards, and the growth of the plant slows up naturally, the tuber itself begins to develop and ripen.

This process goes on for a couple of months or so toward the end of which time, the leaves discolour and fall naturally. While this is happening, moisture should always be available at the roots. The leaves must not be allowed to wilt, otherwise they will endeavour to obtain the moisture required by the tuber, which will suffer as a result, and the following season's flowers may very well be affected.

Most pot begonias retain their foliage until early November and under normal conditions watering will be required until that time.

When the growing season is finished begonias must not be neglected, but encouraged to become dormant in the normal way. The period of dormancy is important since it is during that time that the tubers recover from the exhausting processes of flowering. These annual resting times ensure that the tubers have a good long life and remain vigorous.

It is however, a mistake to suddenly withhold water when it is evident that no more flowers will be produced. Faulty ripening results in a poor show the following season. So long as the foliage remains a good colour, watering should be continued and the plant not forced to go to rest. It is important to let the plant itself show signs of its approaching resting period.

When the lower leaves become discoloured and fall off and no new growth is being made, then is the time to reduce the water supply. Never cut down the plant until this happens. It is only after the flowering period and during the natural dying down of the leaves, that the tuber, which has been hard worked during the flowering season, is able to build up strength for the following season's growth, and to increase in size.

Where the dormancy period is hastened, the corms will not increase in size. They become weak and may be very slow to start into growth the following season. In the autumn, the plant forms layers of spongy tissues at the leaf and stem junctions which prevents sap activity. This in turn, is the natural cause of the leaves becoming yellow and falling off.

The proper procedure, once the plant shows signs of resting, is to cut top growth down to within eight or nine inches from the base. The plants can then be taken out of their pots without removing the soil, and placed in a corner of the greenhouse under the staging, where they are not likely to be subjected to drips of water. After a short time of this treatment, the remaining stalks will drop off or can easily be removed, but do not break them off before they are ready.

Then clean the tubers, making sure that all traces of the old stem and leaves are removed. If left, they may encourage the setting up of decay. When the tuber is cleaned it should be quite firm and plump. Any fleshy roots still adhering, should be left. If the tubers are then lightly dusted with D.D.T. this will prevent pests from settling on them and doing damage during the dormant period.

Concerning the storage conditions, these are not critical and several different methods may be adopted. Wherever the corms are kept, they must always be protected from frost. They must not however, be subjected to hot, dry conditions or they will shrivel and become soft.

Ideally, the storage conditions should be such to ensure that the tubers remain firm and plump. They must not, of course, be subjected to dampness. otherwise, the tubers may start into growth before their proper time. If they can be stored in old potting soil, dry peat or silver sand, at a temperature of around 55 degrees, this will ensure their remaining in good order.

If you have to keep the tubers in a shed or garage, they should be examined frequently, for one touch of frost can soon spoil a whole batch of tubers. Even if only one or two are actually initially touched by frost, the subsequent decay will soon spread to others. Once the tubers are really dry, they can, of course, be kept in boxes, seed trays or flower pots, without being covered at all, but burying them in the materials suggested, is really best.

Where a greenhouse or frame is not available it is still possible to grow begonias. Tubers can be obtained in the early spring. They can be boxed or potted in a peaty compost and kept in a shed or other dry outhouse and started in the usual way. It is also possible to plant dormant tubers straight into the ground at the end of April or early May. The exact time for this will largely depend upon the soil situation and weather conditions.

Obviously plants started in this way will not grow so rapidly at first. This is really all to the good, since they will not then be breaking through the soil while there is still a danger from late frosts. While such plants may not be quite as early as those that are boxed and started in heat there will be little or no other difference in the resultant growth and flowering.

For direct planting the site selected should be sheltered and sunny and consist of fairly rich soil. It should be one which does not dry out since, of course, begonias are plants which do like moisture. When these outdoor plants are growing well, it will be helpful to mulch round the plants with some moisture retaining materials such as peat, leaf mould, or old strawy manure.

A really good planting of begonias seen in a prominent place can prove most pleasing. If such plants show signs of running up to flower before they are really established with a good number of leaves, these early flower buds should be nipped out.

In regard to the harvesting of outdoor tubers, they should

not be lifted too soon and as far as possible not until the foliage discolours and begins to fall. The tubers themselves increase in size only when the plants have finished their flowering and active growing period.

Since just a slight touch of frost will not harm the tubers it is usually quite satisfactory to leave the tubers in the soil until well into October. One must, of course, be governed by the season.

Care is advisable when lifting the tubers, which for preference should be done with soil around each specimen. After lifting place the tubers in trays or shallow boxes and stand them in a frost-proof place, the greenhouse staging being ideal. After they have been in this position for some days the foliage will have fallen and the stems easily break away without damaging the tubers in any way. The latter is, of course, most important, for if any attempt is made to pull off the stems before they are ready, the tuber itself may be damaged and the next season's growth adversely affected.

If you grow tuberous begonias in hanging baskets these should be treated in the same way and not be pulled out of the basket before their growing period is over. Neither should water be withheld before the foliage discolours.

When established in the flowering size pot, it is helpful if the plant is knocked out of the pot so that the root system can be seen. Then one can decide whether to feed immediately or to wait a little while. Really healthy plants which are growing well, will after they have been in their final pots for five or six weeks, have roots which have reached the sides of the pots. If this is so when the plant is knocked out, feeding can be started. Subsequently, further feeds can be given at about fourteen day intervals but here again, much depends upon how strongly the plant continues to grow.

A pot bound plant will often produce flowers quickly. This is because of a natural urge to reproduce itself before dying, a happening which occurs with all sorts of plants, including some which may be damaged but not killed immediately.

If buying begonias in pots, it is better to aim for young

specimens, perhaps beginning to show bud. Such plants are not likely to be root bound and should not therefore produce flowers prematurely. In addition, there is a greater and longer pleasure of seeing the plant reach the flowering stage. When the plant is bought in full bloom, it sometimes does not show further colour once the present blooms have passed over, bringing disappointment to the purchaser.

Begonias will always respond to good treatment. Particularly in the case of the tuberous varieties which have large fleshy leaves and good-sized flowers, regular feeding from the time the flower buds begin to open and while they are showing colour, is essential if best results are to be obtained.

As with other plants, it is impossible to give exact rules regarding feeding since other cultural conditions will vary and different varieties react differently to the same type of feeding. Some plants seem able to use quite large quantities of feeding matter and grow well without any sign of coarseness. Others, while taking less food, may produce soft growth and deformed blooms and rapidly become subject to fungus troubles.

Much depends upon the type of food used since some of the artificial brands contain a very high proportion of nitrogen, which although encouraging quick growth, results in flabby stems liable to mildew and rotting. Whatever brand is used, care is necessary in following the makers instructions. So often, growers wanting to be on the generous side and to treat their plants well, increase the recommended dosage. Far from being helpful to the plants, such action is liable to unbalance them bringing about all kinds of troubles.

Never feed a plant which is not growing well. It can be very harmful to apply fertilisers of any kind until the root system is functioning properly and is therefore able to absorb the feeds supplied and use them to an advantage. If one starts with a good soil mixture it will contain all the plant needs until after the final potting.

CHAPTER FOUR

Some Good Double Flowered Varieties

TUBEROUS BEGONIAS have been greatly improved
since the earliest known species were found in the American
Andes more than ninety years ago. Botanically they are
placed in groups, and that known as the Andean group, is
one of the most important of all.

The original species were classified as Begonia tuberhybrida. It is from these white, small flowered species that
the present well known, giant flowered doubles have been
evolved. The pendula and multiflora types have also come
from the original species some of which were found in
situations which we do not usually associate with begonias.

Among these first-known species from which have come
the modern hybrids, are the following:—

B. boliviensis was first collected over a hundred years ago
and was taken in hand by the old and now defunct firm of
Messrs. James Veitch and Sons of Chelsea. This species is
still in cultivation today and makes slender stems of up to
two feet high and it has long narrow, almost lance-shaped
leaves. The small single, rather drooping flowers are bright
scarlet with yellow stainings. Undoubtedly this is one
of the forerunners of the present Begonia pendula varieties.

Begonia Davisii is a good Veitch introduction first made
known ninety years ago. The name commemorates one of
their most successful collectors. This species grows into a
rather tufted plant, the foliage being bluish-green, while the
flowers are a striking orange-scarlet. It is a begonia which
has been much used in the production of the modern multiflora begonias. This is readily understandable when one

29

remembers its strong yet compact growth, attractive leaves and showy flowers.

B. clarkei is another begonia which has been cultivated in this country for well over a century. Coming from Bolivia, it is a little less hardy than some of the others mentioned in this list. It has sturdy upright stems which support branching, deep green leaves. The flowers are rosy-red and inclined to be of pendulus habit. It is believed that this begonia has been instrumental in providing the sturdy upright stem, so prominent in the modern large flowered varieties.

B. cinnabarina is almost non-existent today but it was known in England in the middle of the last century. Records show that the leaves of this begonia are very similar to many of the present-day large flowered tuberous varieties. It may very well be that it has had an important influence on modern sorts. It produces upright flower stems with cinnabar-red flowers of quite good size.

B. octopetala with pink flowers, has been known in Great Britain for 130 years and has been instrumental in producing several good hybrid tuberous sorts although it has not been used as much for breeding purposes as the others mentioned in this list.

B. pearcei arrived in this country just over a hundred years ago, being one of the finds of Richard Pearce a collector well known in the last century. It is of striking appearance, the dark green, velvety foliage being marbled with lighter markings or veinings. The primrose-yellow flowers are small and are produced above the foliage. It is evident that this begonia has been used to produce many of the yellow shades and tones in the modern begonia.

B. rosaeflora is another species found by Richard Pearce. It has biggish, red-edged leaves, the stems also being shaded red. It produces many flowers of which the colour varies from white and pink, to rosy-red.

B. Veitchii is one more of Pearce's finds. This he discovered in Peru. Its almost round, dark green stemless leaves, combine with the vermilion-red flowers, to make an attractive plant. It is of sturdy growth and seems able to withstand lower temperatures than many others.

There are a number of other little known tuberous begonia species which are not in cultivation today. Mention must be made however of the hybrids from the species in the Andean group just mentioned. These include: –

Begonia presoniensis and B. woodmannii both of which are no longer in cultivation.

Begonia sedeni is one of the earliest hybrids, its name commemorating John Seden who was in the propagating department of the famous Veitch firm.

B. chelsoni was the result of another of Seden's crosses while over ninety years ago, B. White Queen was offered by the firm of Henderson.

In old records we find mentioned Begonia lemoinei and Gloire de Nancy. A number of good seedlings were also offered although the majority of these were never named or distributed.

It is not until we come towards the end of the nineteenth century that we find the double hybrids had caught the interest of the general public. This was very largely through the work of F. C. Langdon, the founder of the present day firm of Blackmore and Langdon to whom the begonia world owes so much. We now have double begonias grouped under such descriptive headings as camellia, rose, hollyhock, carnation, paeony and anemone-flowered types, while the colour range, including many art tones and shades, is unbelievably wide.

The exact colour tones of many of the best double flowering begonias are liable to vary a little on account of the composition of the soil. This, of course, is something which is outside the control of the grower. Sometimes the same variety will show a distinct difference in colour tone, even when grown in the same, or nearby gardens. Such varieties may occur where the soil contains an abundance of iron, while a nearby garden has a higher proportion of lime.

Therefore, occasionally when certain varieties, particularly in the pink tones, are grown they may vary. Another factor which has a bearing on the colour, as given in catalogues, is that very few people interpret colours in exactly the same way. This applies to catalogue compilers as well as to gardeners. This fact also accounts for many slightly different catalogue descriptions of the same variety.

The horticultural colour chart as issued by the Royal Horticultural Society, is of course, a standard guide, although many of the colour names as given there, are not in general use, and unless one is able to refer to the colour chart, it does not help.

Although the colours of many of the large flowered double begonias are so bright, and attractive, they are not gaudy, and fit in well with their natural surroundings. Many of them have a particular brightness which lights up the whole garden or greenhouse in which they are growing.

Begonia blooms are made up of a number of separate florets which are unisexual, that is, the centre flower of the group or cluster, is the male bloom, which is almost always flanked on each side by a female flower. The male blooms are most showy while the female flowers are considerably smaller, and almost always of single form. Excepting in cases where seed is required, the female flowers may be removed with advantage, thus avoiding waste of energy. This applies especially to plants being cultivated for exhibition, although the removal of any flowers should be done while they are tiny.

Good Double Flowering Begonias

Alan Clarke, cardinal red, of excellent form.

Alf Edney, a very large pink of good quality.

Ann Rodway, a new picotee with a really bright red edge, on a pure white background.

Aurora, large salmon-orange.

Blithe Spirit, pale pink, of perfect formation. Late.

Brian Langdon. A giant flowered, bright rose-pink.

Charmain, early-flowering, a tall grower. Carries enormous, pure pink flowers.

1. Begonia Semperflorens.

2. Begonia: Fibrous Rooted.

3. Gloxinia Grandiflora, Hybrid.

4. A Free Flowering Hybrid Gloxinia.

5. Saint Paulia Blue Hybrid.

6. Begonia Pendula.

7. Ruffled form of Picotee.

8. An ordinary Ruffled form Begonia.

Clarissa Hutchinson, bright salmon. F.C.C.

Crown Prince is one of the very best and richest crimsons, an improvement even on Royal Duke, with larger, and very freely produced flowers.

Delice, salmon-orange. F.C.C.

Diana Wynyard, very large, pure white. Free-flowering. F.C.C.

El Alamein, vivid crimson.

Everest, white, of good form.

Fantasy, a very beautiful picotee, with a yellow ground colour, and a very fine and clear pink edge. Stronger growing than most members of this group.

Festiva, fine new yellow of a particularly deep chrome shade. Early flowering, and bearing rose-shaped flowers of good size.

Firecrest, heavily crinkled petals of deep bronze-yellow, touched with scarlet.

Flambeau. A very fine orange-scarlet.

Frou-Frou, fine picotee-edged variety with a white ground colour. The flowers are not large, but the deep pink edge, is well defined.

Goldrush, rich chrome-yellow of first-class form and texture. Early, and free flowering.

Guardsman, a most brilliant glorious orange-scarlet, quite outstanding.

Harlequin, the finest picotee begonia we have seen, and indeed one of the most attractive begonias ever raised, fascinating all who see it.

Harmony, free flowering blush-picotee.

Helen Sproull, enormous pink of great depth.

H. Frankling, rich vermilion.

Hilda Langdon, rose pink of good size and shape.

Honeydew, a huge newcomer, which will especially delight exhibitors, producing deep flowers the colour of champagne – a new shade in begonias.

Ivorine, pure cream. Early and lasts well.

Jamboree, a picotee with yellow ground colour and heavily marked, waved petals. Very free flowering.

B

Jean Blair, striking picotee with a rich yellow ground colour and a pronounced scarlet edge.

John Langdon, a rich salmon-rose of fine quality.

John Woolman. A beautiful orange-salmon with slightly overlaid petals.

Ken Macdonald, most attractive orange. Strong grower.

Kismet, a very unusual combination of soft apricot, with a distinctive rose-picotee edge.

Lucy Dare, a really pretty rose-pink.

Lionel Richardson, salmon-orange flowers of perfect size and form.

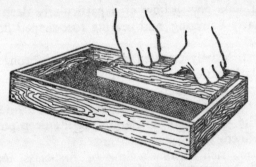

Firming soil before sowing or transplanting

Margaret Collins, a glorious clear pink. Especially suitable for show work, combines enormous flowers, with excellent keeping qualities.

Marjorie Porton, white; waved petals.

Midas, glorious golden yellow of great depth and quality. One of the finest yellows.

Mildred Butler, cream shading to primrose. Fine for exhibition.

Moonlight, creamy-yellow, of fine form and habit.

Mrs. T. N. Waldron, salmon-cerise, with a really good centre.

Ninette, the most delightful shade of palest salmon-apricot, which we believe to be a new colour. They are very large flowers, freely produced and lasting well.

N. F. Barnes, large rich orange.

N. M. Agnew, a grand yellow variety.

Olympia, brilliant crimson-scarlet, the effect being enhanced by the pronounced marking of the foliage.

Prelude, grand new pink, which produces large flowers of considerable depth.

Primrose, a fine and pleasing primrose-yellow.

Rebecca, striking clear sugar-pink, of perfect rosebud shape.

Rhapsody, very large salmon-pink; exquisite quality and free. F.C.C.

Rosanna, fine deep rose-coloured variety, the colour being slightly paler in the centre. Exceptionally free flowering.

Rose Edney, a large crimson-scarlet.

Royal Duke, superb crimson of wonderful texture and quality. A very fine, free flowering plant.

Roy Hartley, enormous flowered soft pink, tinged with salmon. One of the very finest varieties.

Salmonea, salmon-orange self.

Sam Phillips, a first-class yellow of high quality.

Sir Phillip Sassoon, a fine crimson with full centre.

Sugar Candy, may be regarded as a development of Roy Hartley, being a clearer pink, and a good deal earlier flowering. A delightful variety in every way.

Sunray, free flowering, light orange.

Sylph, medium yellow of good form. Vigorous.

T. B. Toop, bright orange, of perfect form.

W. J. Naish, rich orange shading.

Zephyr, cream bicolour, shading to blush.

Buttermilk (new). Extra large rose-shaped cream coloured flowers.

Elaine Fanttelin (new). Deep rose pink. Slightly serrated petals.

Mary Heatley (new). Huge flowers of warm golden-orange.

Recent work by hybridists has resulted in the introduction of several new strains of double begonias. One of the most attractive of these is known as Crown Jewels. This produces shapely plants containing perfectly proportioned full double rose-shaped flowers in a wide range of beautiful pastel shades including cerise, pink, salmon, apricot, orange, yellow and white.

In order to secure seeds of these double strains special care is needed. Double flowers are of course sterile and have to be discarded when the plants are being grown for seed. It is only the single male and female flowers which are retained for pollinating. One can realise why seed of such strains of begonias is expensive to buy, since it is not unusual for up to 200 plants growing in five-inch pots, to produce between them only one ounce of seed. The seed is of course extremely minute and what seems to be a small quantity actually consists of a very large number of individual seeds.

Seed sown in January or February will produce plants which begin to bloom early in July and many individual plants in this mixed strain equal some of the best named varieties in regard to size, shape and colour.

CHAPTER FIVE

Rex and other Rhizomatous Sorts

THE RHIZOMATOUS species are an important and large section of the begonia family. The tuberous species are, of course, grown for their flowers, but in this section, the plants are cultivated because of their highly ornamental foliage. They come chiefly from America and Asia. Their particular habit of growth is governed in the way the roots form. Some develop along the surface of the soil, making bushy plants which are not usually difficult to divide. The habit of some species is low growing and almost horizontal. These do not send down deep roots. Others are of more upright growth. It is not possible to include all the species, but the following are among the best, Rex probably being the most important.

Some of them are a little difficult to secure without searching for them.

B. boweri, a fairly recent introduction from Mexico. This is a small growing species, with dark green leaves having deep brown markings along the edges.

B. heracleifolia, has been known for a very long time. It forms creeping rhizomes, from which erupt star-shaped leaves, of which the hairy stalks are attractively spotted red. Apart from the green-leaved type, there are a number of varieties with bronze or blackish markings.

B. imperialis is another miniature variety known for well over a century. It has rich green, plush-like leaves, which are prettily marked with darker green and brown. There are a number of varieties of this species, all with attractive markings, and with raised spots or pimples on the foliage, which are an added attraction.

B. kenworthyi produces pointed, lobed, bluish-green leaves of upright habit.

B. manicata is probably the best known of the American species and it has long been grown in this country. The smooth green leaves have numerous, thick red hairs at the base. The variety aureo-maculata has foliage marked yellow and pink, while the leaves of another variety, crispa, are handsomely ruffled. There are also a number of other varieties of manicata, which have a number of attractive ways.

B. manicata has been used with other species as a parent and a number of attractive varieties have been produced, many having the good points of the species as well as many other attributes.

Another American rhizomatous begonia, is the hybrid, B. Silver Star, of which the shining silver leaves are markedly pointed.

Of the asiatic rhizomatous begonias, only a few are in general cultivation and here again, they are not easy to obtain. Some of them require a fair amount of warmth. The following are among the easiest and most likely to be obtainable from specialist suppliers.

B. handelii, has bright green leaves with attractive reddish hairs. The light pink flowers are nicely scented.

B. masoniana Iron Cross was brought to this country by Mr. L. Maurice Mason of Kings Lynn in 1952. The large leaves are attractively pimpled, while the bright green blades have deep brown markings in the shape of an iron cross. It is not difficult to manage and is rapidly increasing in favour. Easily propagated from leaf cuttings, it is undoubtedly one of the most pleasing of recent introductions.

B. smithiae has been known in Britain for almost forty years. This plant has leaves of rusty-red tinged pink. Established plants usually bear orange coloured flowers.

B. versicolour is another begonia of fairly recent introduction. Not unlike B. Iron Cross, the emerald green leaves are shaded a delightful silvery-green with dark mahogany-brown veins. This begonia is of value not only for its attrac-

tive appearance but because of its use as a parent in hybridising.

Rex begonias are among the most beautiful of all foliage
plants. The original plant was found in Assam, well over a
century ago. Because of its wonderful markings, it was given
its present name of Begonia rex (or rex celtosum) which of
course, literally means King of Begonias.

This plant has heart-shaped leaves which are a metallic
bluish-green colour, with broad silvery-white markings right
round the leaf, about an inch from the margin. It is stemless
and produces an underground rhizome immediately. The
beauty of the leaves of this plant caused much attention,
and hybridists were not slow to realise the possibilities.

A considerable amount of crossing was carried out with
other species and some of the hybrids produced proved to be
larger, taller plants which did not require such warm growing
conditions. Other crossings resulted in small leaved varieties
being produced and still others gave plants of a different leaf
shape. Just over seventy years ago, continual hybridising
brought about plants having a greatly extended colour range
in their foliage, including many bronze, red and bluish
shades, all with a metallic beauty.

Then early this century, the species B. cathayana was
used in crossing. This species has velvety leaves which are
emerald green with a silvery-green zone and wine coloured
veins. The undersides of the leaves are also beautifully
coloured. This species is one of the most handsome of all
and it was certainly a happy combination in uniting it with
Begonia rex.

Subsequently, other species have been used with Rex, and
this has resulted in the production of a number of separate
sections of Rex hybrids. Not only has the colour range been
increased and intensified but apart from the large leaved,
stemless rex varieties, there are sorts having upright, branching or tree habit, spiral leaved and miniature ' tree ', and
miniature spiral sorts.

The varied colours of the Rex varieties are sometimes
influenced by cultural conditions. Apart from the named

forms, there are many unnamed varieties available. In addition, it is believed that some of the older sorts have been sent out under different names.

Among the sorts which are in cultivation at the present time the following are among the best on account of their most colourful leaves and good habit.

Large and medium leaved varieties: Aberconway, Eau-de-Nil, Gloire-des-Ardennes, La France, Queen Victoria, Remilly and Silver Queen.

Among the finest spiral leaved sorts are: Bronze King, Curly Fireflush, Princess of Hanover, and Twisty Spot.

Of the upright branching sorts, there are: Abel Carrieré, Filigree, Mrs. Hoffman, Pinkie and Silver Sweet.

Of the miniature leaved Rex varieties: Baby Rainbow, Dewdrop, Peacock and Silver Fleece are excellent, although not easy to find at the present time.

Among the attractive miniature leaves ' tree ' sorts are Diana Bedson and Tapestry, while there is a similar leaved ' tree ' spiral variety, known as Brown Curl, which is well worth hunting for, although it is rarely offered in catalogues.

Rex begonias can be propagated from both stem and leaf cuttings. The former method is the quickest and can be done at any time when the plant is in full growth, and the sap is active. For good results, the cuttings should be rooted in a warm propagating frame with, for preference, bottom heat of about 70 degrees F. Shade and a close atmosphere are helpful, with sufficient ventilation to discourage any tendency to rotting off. Although a steady temperature and a moist atmosphere is needed, dank, stagnant conditions will cause trouble.

Perhaps the most simple method of increasing Rex begonias, is by rooting leaves. The right conditions for this are provided by using a propagating frame, and if this can stand on the greenhouse bench, and have bottom heat by means of soil warming cables, so much the better.

There are several good rooting mediums, including a mixture of peat and sand, or leaf mould and sand. Many growers find that clean silver sand alone is quite satisfactory, others depend upon vermiculite. This, however, does not seem quite so satisfactory as sand or peat.

Select really good healthy, well marked leaves, and lay them flat on the surface of pots, pans or boxes of the chosen rooting medium, making sure that a short length of leaf stem has also been buried. The whole leaf can be pegged down flat and then the junctions or joints of the main veins can be severed. If the surface is kept just moist, new plantlets will soon grow from each of the cut vein junctions. In the case of very big leaves the margins or edges can be trimmed off so that there is less loss of moisture by evaporation.

Another method is to actually cut out portions of the leaves complete with a good vein, and to insert these firmly, preferably at an angle, as is done with ordinary cuttings. Although moisture must not be lacking on the surface of the sand, water must not settle on the upper leaf surface. If it does, decay and similar troubles may occur. Once the little leaf cuttings are well rooted they can be potted up separately in the usual way.

Apart from Begonia rex, other ornamental leaved begonia species in cultivation, some of which are mentioned elsewhere, are : –

B. albo-picta. Greenish-white, foliage glossy green spotted silver, 1–1½ ft. Brazil.

B. alleryi. Red and white, 3–4 ft. (hybrid).

B. argenteo-guttata. White and pink, foliage speckled with white. 2–4 ft. (hybrid).

B. bowringiana. See laciniata.

B. heracleifolia. White or rose, foliage deeply lobed. 2–4 ft. (hybrid).

B. imperialis. White, foliage deep velvety green and bright green. 6–12 inches. Mexico.

B. laciniata (syn. B. bowringiana). White, foliage purplish-black and green. 1½–2 ft. India and China.

B. maculata. Rose or white, foliage green dotted white. 2–4 ft. Brazil.

B*

B. metallica. Blush-white, foliage green with metallic lustre. 3–4 ft. Brazil.

B. olbia. White, foliage bronze-green dotted white. 1 ft. Brazil.

B. ricinifolia. Rose-pink, foliage lobed, bronze-green. 2–4 ft. (hybrid).

B. sanguinea. White, foliage rich green above, blood-red beneath. 4 ft. Brazil.

The following is a summary of some of the rhizomatous species, many of which are not easy to obtain at the present time but are well worth searching for:—

American Species:

Begonia boweri was discovered in Mexico less than twenty years ago. Its small, rich green leaves having deep brown markings near the edge.

B. hepatica-maculata was brought from Mexico about fourteen years ago. The thickish, bright green leaves are prettily marked with reddish-brown.

B. heracleifolia was first discovered in Mexico more than 135 years ago. The star-shaped, green leaves are carried on reddish stems. There would appear to be several forms, some having leaves marked or blotched with black or bronze. This species has been used with others to produce a number of useful hybrids.

B. imperialis is a rather tender but attractive, small growing begonia found in Mexico well over a century ago. In some ways, it is similar to Begonia rex and undoubtedly this species has been used with Rex, to produce a number of varieties. B. imperialis has several forms and is also responsible for a number of attractive hybrids.

B. kenworthyi came from Mexico fifteen years or so ago. Of upright habit, it has ivy-shaped leaves of bluish-green.

B. manicata is one of the best known of the American rhizomatous species and has in fact, been popular for 130 years or so. It produces rather twisting rhizomes, from which develop plain green leaves. These have a cluster of red hairs near the base of the leaf blades. There are a number of varieties of this species which has been used to produce several attractive hybrids, some of which have frilled edges to their leaves.

Asiatic Species:

B. goegoensis is a handsome species requiring really warm conditions since it comes from Sumatra. The dark green, roundish leaves are lit up with reddish marks and veinings.

B. Iron Cross was brought to this country by Mr. Maurice Mason. The bright green leaves have brown markings more or less in the shape of a cross and the surface of the leaves is raised or pimpled. An easy variety to grow, it can be readily increased from leaf cuttings.

B. handelii. Although this has been known for forty-five years or so, it is only during the last thirteen years that it has become at all well known in this country. The bright green leaves are freely adorned with reddish hairs, while the light pink flowers have a pleasing perfume.

B. versicolor was brought to Britain from China about fifteen years ago. In some respects, it is rather like B. Iron Cross, having deep brownish-red markings on its silvery-green leaves. It is said to have been used successfully for crossing with a number of other species resulting in some good hybrids.

CHAPTER SIX

Begonia Semperflorens

THEIR EASE of culture and continuous flowering ability have made the semperflorens begonias most popular.
The original species B. semperflorens has given its name to
a group of varieties which has resulted from a union of this
species with several others. These hybrids have a glossy
foliage which accounts for the name Wax begonias by which
the group is sometimes known. Furthermore all the varieties
have the ability to flower continuously, and in fact, it is
this quality which gives rise to the group name which simply
put, means ' always flowering '. It is not always realised
that Begonia semperflorens will flower in the winter, if plants
are lifted from the open ground in late September and potted
up, they will flower intermittently for many weeks. Even
when there are no flowers the coloured foliage makes them
quite ornamental subjects.

B. semperflorens itself, which is difficult to find nowadays,
has white, slightly tinged pink flowers, and pale green, shiny
foliage. The variation in the size of the semperflorens varieties is of course, due to the influence of the different parents
used, some hybrids having quite tall stems as opposed to the
short, compact growth of others.

The colour range too, has become quite wide, both in
regard to leaves and to the flowers. There are some sorts
with almost variegated leaves and at least one, with yellowish
leaves. Others have bronze-red or dark red foliage, while
there are a few which have white leaves, of a shape which
has caused them to be described as the Calla leaved
begonias.

There are a number of very good double flowered sorts

as well as a wide range of single varieties. The colour range is extensive, but although there is a record of a variety with yellow flowers having been raised over fifty years ago, this colour is not available today. There is no difficulty in regard to raising begonia semperflorens from seed. The main point to observe is that the young plants must be kept growing vigorously for if they do sustain a check of any kind, such as the drying out of the compost even for a short period, they take some time to recover.

Seed is sown very early in March in prepared trays of soil of which the top must be very fine. The John Innes Seed Compost is frequently used, but any sweet, fine, soil mixture is suitable. When prepared for sowing, the trays should be well watered so that the compost is uniformly moist. The seed is dust-like, and therefore, needs to be sown with great care. This is best done by spreading it very thinly over the surface of the trays, but because of the fineness of the seed, no attempt should be made to cover it.

Some growers have found it easier to sow the seed evenly, by mixing it with fine silver sand and then spreading it over the surface. I have not found this altogether satisfactory for so often the tiny seed remains in clusters in the sand, resulting in a ' gappy ' box when the seedlings appear.

After sowing, give the trays a very light watering with a fine rosed can, and then cover them with glass and paper, which will greatly help in preventing the compost from drying out.

If kept where the temperature is from 60 to 65 degrees F. the seed will normally germinate in a few days. As soon as the first signs of growth are visible, the glass and paper should be removed. It is from this time that special care must be taken to make sure that the soil does not dry out. Since the seedlings are so small and delicate, it is almost impossible to handle them singly at the stage when they should be moved from the sowing trays. It is therefore advisable to carry out the operation known to nurserymen as ' patching off '. This simply means that little groups of seedlings are pricked out or ' patched off ' into other trays where they remain until they are big enough to handle singly.

This job requires both patience and skill and is best done with a label or pronged stick. With these, groups of about six seedlings are lifted from their positions and transferred to other prepared trays in which little depressions are made in the soil and the little plants placed in them. See that the soil around the seedlings and that in the trays, is brought into close contact, so that there is no danger of the little plants dying because of their tiny roots drying out.

Once the seedlings in the groups have grown big enough to handle separately, they can be moved individually to trays the standard size accommodating fifty-four plants. When further growth has been made, the plants can be moved to the three-inch size pots where they will flower well, although subsequently bigger plants can be moved again to five-inch pots.

For the past sixty or seventy years hybrids of real value have been continually introduced, and in listing names, it is well realised that some good ones will of necessity be omitted in order to keep within the space available.

The following may be depended upon as being among the very best of the single varieties:–

Calla Lily. Pink flowers with unusually coloured leaves which are almost white towards the top, the lower part being pale green.

Carmen. A popular cerise with bronzy-purple leaves.

Crimson Bedder. Bright scarlet-crimson, dark foliage.

Fireball. Miniature growing, bright scarlet flowers, dark leaves.

Loveliness. Light pink, green foliage.

Rose Queen. Carmine-pink, green leaves.

Snowball. Small growing, white flowers, green foliage.

Tausendschon. Rose-pink, green leaves.

Winter Romance, Dwarf, carmine-pink, green foliage.

Reliable double flowering sorts, include the following:–

Calla Lily Double. Pink, with green and white foliage.

Gustav Lund. Pink, light green leaves.

Pink Camellia. Pink, bronzy-red foliage.

Robin Hood. Pink, dark centre, bronze leaves.

Thimbleberry. Red and yellow, dark foliage.

There does not appear to be a yellow flowered variety in cultivation today, but a form known as Golden King is said to have been available seventy years ago.

During the last few years a number of Begonia semperflorens F. I. Hybrids have been developed. These have proved to be a great improvement on the older sorts. They have hybrid vigour, showing great resistance to adverse weather conditions and are proving to be first-class in every way. The improvement of most of the older varieties, all are excellent for bedding and pot work.

Begonia semperflorens have never been so popular. in this country as on the continent. This is probably because the older varieties did not really like our climate. The new F. I. Hybrids are resistant to humid and other adverse conditions and show signs of becoming very popular indeed.

The following are particularly good, most growing five or six-inches high : –

Andy, small neat plants covered with large, deep coral-pink flowers.

Lucifer, rich scarlet flowers showing up well among shining almost black foliage. This variety which grows nine to ten inches high, has received an Award of Merit from the R.H.S.

Organdy, a mixture of many colours giving a particularly gay effect.

Pandy, similar to Andy but with bright orange-scarlet flowers.

Rosa Rheingauperle, bright rose-pink.

Sleeping Beauty, bright carmine flowers freely produced. An excellent sun and rain-proof variety.

Thousand Wonders, a fine pink sort of compact habit.

Red Thousand Wonders, a splendid red form of the previous variety.

Thousand Wonders Rose and Thousand Wonders White

are other fine forms, of neat habit and very effective for bedding.

Whiskey, pure white flowers contrasting with the shiny bronze foliage. This has been given awards at Wisley and the Horticultural Show in Hamburg in 1963.

Red Comet produces medium large sized scarlet flowers on compact plants, which have purplish-red foliage.

Pink Comet is an attractive light salmon-pink, producing an abundance of lovely bronzy-green foliage.

Rose Comet has deep rose blooms, on well-shaped plants, which have reddish-bronze leaves.

White Comet is particularly free flowering, the bronzy-green leaves contrasting well with the pure white blooms.

The Galaxy F.I. Hybrids produce multitudes of medium sized, starry flowers in a well balanced colour range, the foliage of all being purplish or bronzy. The plant habit is very even, and under ordinary normal conditions each specimen makes a compact plant six or seven inches high.

All of these can be sown in December or January, and by the following May, they will be splendid plants ready for potting or setting out in the open. A July sowing will produce plants for blooming in December.

When sowing the seed use light compost containing plenty of organic matter. As with other begonias, the seeds should be sown very thinly on a surface of moist compost, no covering at all being necessary. Then apply a fine moist spray, and cover the tray or box with a sheet of glass until the germination occurs. If the plants are kept under cool conditions, it will bring out the leaf colourings very effectively. It can be reckoned that sixteen to eighteen weeks will elapse from the time of sowing the seeds until the plants are ready to start flowering.

A whole series of Tom Thumb varieties of Begonia semperflorens is now available. These are first-class for summer bedding as well as for growing in pots in the greenhouse. The majority grow four or five inches high and are therefore ideal for edging and can be used with great effect for carpet bedding. The following are among the best:–

Dainty Maid: deep pink buds, opening to pure white flowers edged pink, the deep green foliage being edged bronze.

Fireball: bright carmine-scarlet with frilly foliage.

Fire King: vivid fiery scarlet, the olive-green foliage being prettily marked with silver.

Indian Maid: this is a dwarf form of the taller growing variety of the same name. It makes really bushy plants, the scarlet flowers showing up well against the bronzy foliage.

Karen: the pure white flowers contrasting with the dark leaves.

Matador: bright scarlet with green foliage, forming a compact plant.

Pink Comet: salmon-pink on bronzy green foliage.

Pink Miniature: a particularly fine dwarf sort with showy rose-pink flowers.

Scarlet Ball: showy scarlet blooms, the deep green foliage being shaded bronze.

Snowball: pure white with light green leaves. Of excellent habit.

W. Seeger: large red flowers with dark foliage.

All of these can be raised from seed without difficulty.

CHAPTER SEVEN

Begonia Gloire de Lorraine

A GREAT favourite during Victorian times. and now
rapidly coming into favour again. Begonia Gloire de
Lorraine, is a remarkable hybrid. It is the result of crossing
Begonia socotrana and other species.

As a pot plant, it will bloom well under widely differing
temperatures, although 60 degree F. and plenty of atmospheric moisture may be considered as the ideal conditions.

This is one of the best winter flowering plants, which will
give a full six weeks display. It is constant changes in
temperature which sometimes cause both the leaves and
flowers to drop prematurely. Since the blooms are sterile,
the plants cannot be raised from seed, but fortunately, plenty
of shoots suitable for making cuttings are produced.

Neither a tuberous rooted or fibrous rooted subject, this
plant actually produces a thickish rooting system, which
enables it to come through the winter. In order to secure
first-class cuttings, it is advisable to cut back the shoots to
half their length. Do this immediately after flowering and
then in the early spring, when new growth is visible. cut the
stems back further. This will result in the propagation of
strong basal shoots. ideal for propagating. These may be
inserted in trays or boxes of sandy soil. under the propagating frame. The placing of several cuttings in each small pot
seems to give the quickest and best results.

Vermiculite is sometimes used. but this is of course. completely sterile, so that potting up must be done immediately
the roots have formed. A good temperature for rooting the
cuttings is about 65 degrees F. which should be lowered to
60 degrees once the cuttings have been potted off. Early

rooted specimens quickly branch out and obviously the first rooted plants will break out most, and develop into the biggest, bushiest specimens. Flower buds will appear on the newly rooted cuttings and should be kept most regularly rubbed out.

Keep the young begonias growing sturdily in three-inch pots of John Innes No. 2 or a similar compost and avoid both a hot, dry atmosphere, and draughts. Once the pots are full of roots, move to bigger receptacles, working in the

Well rooted begonia tuber, ready for potting in

soil carefully but do not ram the roots for they break easily. Avoid anything likely to cause a check. When the plants are growing well, they will need light supports. For this the tips of bamboo canes are ideal.

Insert them carefully but securely, for the stems bruise easily. The special soft twine available should be used in the tying. If the ties are made just above the lowest flower buds on the stem, they will be almost invisible, an important point when plants are used in the living-room.

If some kind of organic liquid fertiliser is given, from the time the plants are half grown, it will lead to really sturdy well developed plants. The flowering period can be regulated, which is fortunate, when one wishes to have plants in bloom at a specific time. About six weeks elapses between the time the flower buds are first seen until they are fully open.

By careful planning and dis-budding, it is possible to have fine flowering specimens available over a period of six to eight weeks, which is something which cannot be said of every flowering plant. While the original hybrids had pink flowers others have been produced in different colours, some having reddish or bronze foliage. Some of the original Lorraine hybrids have been crossed back on to Begonia socotrana, so that there is now another interesting range available.

Of the older sorts, Mrs. Leopold de Rothschild, with pink flowers is most reliable; and Turnford Hall is white flushed apple-blossom pink. Other good hybrids include: Ege's Favourite, which has large deep pink flowers; Mrs. J. A. Peterson, is deep pink with bronzy leaves; while Sunbank is another rich pink of upright habit with fleshy, veined leaves.

CHAPTER EIGHT

Winter Flowering Varieties

WHERE A warm greenhouse is available winter flowering begonias will provide a really bright colourful display. The most popular is Gloire de Lorraine and its varieties. Raised by the celebrated French plant breeder, Victor Lemoine nearly seventy-seven years ago, Gloire de Lorraine was the result of crossing B. Socotrana and B. Dregei. The former species produces rose-pink flowers in the winter. The latter is a tuberous species, not of any great striking beauty but remarkable for the fact that it has been used successfully to develop several valuable types of begonias.

Although both parents have a semi-bulbous or semi-tuberous root habit, Gloire de Lorraine has a fibrous root system. It remains in growth throughout the year but it has a definite resting period in the spring and early summer, when the fresh growth is made. The original hybrid had numerous pink flowers but subsequent varieties have been produced in other shades besides which, some sorts have rich reddish or bronze foliage.

Among the older but still obtainable, good sorts, are Turnford Hall, a white, flushed apple blossom sort, and Mrs. Leopold de Rothschild, a reliable variety which is an improved form of the original Gloire de Lorraine, having slightly paler but larger flowers.

A further development was the crossing back of the Lorraine hybrids on to B. Socotrana. This was successful and has resulted in a range of varieties having larger leaves and good sized single flowers. Among the varieties available are :—

Ege's Favourite, with large deep pink flowers.

Koope's Surprise, rich deep pink almost red.

Lady Mac, a lovely sort with clear pink flowers.

Mrs. J. A. Peterson, deep pink with rich bronzy leaves.

Sunbank, deep pink, upright flowers and fleshy, veined leaves.

White Silence, a really first-class white variety.

Some years ago the Lorraine varieties were given the group name of Cheimantha to distinguish them from other winter flowering begonias although this title is rarely used by the average horticulturist.

To achieve success with this type of begonia, it is essential to provide a temperature not lower than 55 degrees F. although when the plants are being started into new growth ten degrees higher is desirable. The reason that difficulties sometimes arise in the propagation of these plants is that insufficient heat is available. With the right amount of warmth their culture is not beyond the skill of the ordinary grower of greenhouse plants.

So often these begonias are taken into the living-room for table decoration, and because of the very great difference in temperature, as a result of this sudden excursion, the flowers and sometimes the leaves too, fall off very quickly.

Lorraine begonias produce sterile flowers and cannot therefore, be raised from seed, so that it is necessary to start by securing strong plants from a specialist nursery. June being a good month to purchase stock. As the plants develop, they should be moved from the three-inch pots in which they will be purchased to the six or seven-inch size in which they will normally commence to flower in October. Use a good sweet compost made up of 3 parts loam, 1 part each of leaf mould, silver sand and decayed manure, plus a good sprinkling of bone meal, and a little charcoal.

If more convenient, the John Innes Potting Compost No. 2 may be used. Keep the plants growing in a warm, moist, but buoyant atmosphere and see that they are supported as necessary, but do this so as to retain the natural elegant appearance of the plants. In this connection it is advisable to pinch out the growing points as required, to keep the plants of good shape. Furthermore, the removing of some, or all of the flower buds from time to time, does enable the flowering period to be delayed until any particular time required. If buds appear in October and are removed, the flowers will then develop in November or December on-wards, when of course, they are particularly valuable.

Once the flower buds are developing, the plant will be greatly helped by applications of liquid manure at ten day intervals, but keep away from quick acting, artificial fer-tilisers which, if used often, lead to bud dropping and irre-gular development.

Properly looked after, a three-year-old plant will present an imposing appearance and prove to be a real joy during the winter months, when flowers are less plentiful. The flowering season extends from October until February, after which the plants are rested by being kept partially dry in a cooler part of the house. The stems will remain active so that although only a very little moisture is applied to the soil in the pots during the resting period, a very dry atmos-phere must be avoided. After some weeks of resting the plants are brought into a warmer moist environment and the growths are cut down to about half their height, taking care to make each cut immediately above a joint. Soon new shoots will appear and these must have all possible light, without being exposed to the direct sunlight.

Once they are growing strongly, larger pots should be provided and subsequently the tips of the shoots must be pinched out and this should be repeated at intervals as necessary to secure shapely plants of bushy habit. Regular attention must also be given to staking and tying. It is also a good plan to turn the pots round at frequent intervals, to encourage even growth, while from this time, applications of liquid manure can be given and any early or premature blooms can be removed, especially if the plants are wanted to flower at a particular time.

Propagation presents no difficulty to the average grower, for the varieties in the Lorraine group increase readily from cuttings taken from the terminal growths of the stems and branches. These should be secured at a length of about four inches and be prepared in the usual way by making a straight cut immediately below a joint. Remove the lower leaves and any flower buds and insert the cuttings in a sandy, peaty soil mixture. Ideally the cuttings should be rooted in a propagating frame where there is bottom heat, and where there is a temperature of about 65 degrees F. Where such convenience is available, propagation can be carried out from the end of November onwards. Otherwise, the cuttings are best taken in the spring using the new growths which are developing from the base or from the fresh growths higher up the stems.

Begonia socotrana has had a great influence in the production of another group of winter flowering hybrids, for crossed with the tuberous rooted Andean species, it has given rise to the hiemalis varieties. As this group name signifies they are winter flowering and the blooms produced are most beautiful. There are single, semi-double and double forms. The colour range is wide and although there is none of the bronzy-red shading in the leaves, such as appears in the Lorraines, the foliage is most attractive.

It is seventy-five years since the first hiemalis begonia was raised, and since then many fine varieties have been introduced, first by the old firm of Messrs. James Veitch and subsequently by several others, notably Clibrans of Altrincham.

It is a great pity that the latter firm have ceased to concentrate on these fibrous rooted winter flowering begonias. They were the raisers of such excellent varieties as Altrincham Pink, with double rose-pink flowers, Clibran's Pink, another double deep pink and Emily Clibran, a rich rose-pink, of which the centres of the double flowers are of a camellia-like appearance.

These sorts are still available today along with Baard's Wonder, bright red; single; Exquisite a large single with pale pink flowers; Fascination, a popular, dependable single salmon-orange; Flambeau, semi-double, orange-scarlet; Optima, a single, small flowered but reliable salmon-orange;

Orange King, a large single, orange-yellow, suffused pale pink; President, double, rosy-red; Rose Queen, semi-double, rose pink, shaded red, and Snowdrop, a good double white.

All flower from October until the New Year. They are first-class pot plants, although they really require more continuous warmth than can be provided in an ordinary living-room. These begonias can be retained from season to season and they are very often used annually as house plants for their flowering period, or they can then be discarded or given to someone who has suitable greenhouse room available.

It is usually possible to obtain plants in three-inch pots in July and sometimes bigger specimens in five-inch pots can be bought in September. Most plants will make good bushy growth so that they may be given a six or seven-inch pot as their final move.

A temperature of around 55 degrees F. will suit the plants, and when early flower buds appear it is best to keep them nipped out, for the blooms are most valuable from October onwards. Young plants purchased early should be stopped when they have reached a height of six to eight inches so as to induce bushiness. Further stopping should be done as necessary, bearing in mind that it is a good shapely specimen which is the most decorative.

Occasional feeds of liquid manure will result in good sturdy growth which will carry plenty of flowers. A watch must be kept for pests, although they are very rarely troublesome if the plants are grown under healthy conditions. So long as there are no flowers, the easiest way of destroying thrip, begonia mite or aphis, is to dip the entire plant in a good insecticide.

Supports will be necessary as growth develops and should be given at an early stage, for once the stems have grown tall, and in a certain position, it will be almost impossible to alter their direction of growth and they may break if any attempt is made to do so.

The general culture of the hiemalis begonias is exactly the same as that needed by the Lorraines. With both, the critical time is immediately after the flowering period, which is from the end of January until the beginning of April when a partial rest is required.

It will be sufficient if a temperature just over 40 degrees F. is provided then and although some moisture is necessary, only a little is needed; just enough to keep the leaves on and the stems plump.

It is the art of giving just the right amount of water which determines how well the plants will do the following season. Too much may lead to rotting off; too little may make it difficult for the plants to start into growth at the end of April. Even when great care is taken some leaves are almost certain to fall and with some varieties, notably Optima, the stems may become entirely denuded of foliage during the resting spell. Once the new growth commences a certain amount of pinching back or the entire removal of some shoots is usually necessary, in order to keep the plants to the desired shape. Some of these shoots can be retained as cuttings if required. and those of about three inches long can be trimmed in the usual way and inserted in pots or pans of sandy loam. If they can be kept in a propagator where there is a temperature of 70 degrees F. they will not be difficult to strike. It is of course, also possible to obtain good young rooted cuttings without a propagator, although for good results a temperature of between 60 and 70 degrees F. is required. Cuttings taken in June normally make really large exhibition size plants by December, but later struck cuttings, while making nice bushy plants, will only need the three or five-inch pots according to the growth made.

All winter flowering begonias like a moist atmosphere but should not be sprayed overhead. The frequent damping down of floor and staging will usually provide the right growing conditions. It is difficult in a small greenhouse to prevent the air becoming hot and dry during the summer, but a lot can be done by applying some kind of shading to the glass. If there is the convenience, it is quite satisfactory to move the pots to the cold frame during midsummer and if plunged in peat or weathered ashes and shaded from direct sunshine, they will develop freely during the summer.

Occasionally hiemalis begonias will, when several years old, form thickened, almost tuberous roots which can be treated like the ordinary tuberous begonias by being dried off in January and restarted in warmth in April.

CHAPTER NINE

Small Flowered Begonias

Pendula or Basket varieties

A most useful and interesting section of the begonia family is that known as the pendula or basket group. The origin of this type is a little uncertain although, it seems almost certain that the species B. boliviensis was largely used in bringing this class into being. The correct name of the pendula begonias is B. tuberhybrida pendula.

There are both single and double forms, the latter first being brought to notice towards the end of the last century under the name of B. chrysanthemiflora. This was fifteen years or so after the single type had been cultivated, chiefly in France. When they were introduced into the United States, it was under the name of Begonia Lloydii, a title now known to be without authority.

Pendula begonias require the same treatment as the usual tuberous-rooted type, excepting that they are normally grown in wire or similar hanging baskets, instead of ordinary pots. They can, of course, be grown in pots, particularly when they are needed for draping the front of the greenhouse staging or they can stand in the front of window boxes so that the growths hang down.

The graceful trailing stems are furnished with smallish, pointed leaves and a real abundance of small pendula flowers, which together, when in full growth, completely hide the containers in which the plants are growing. With these begonias, the aim should be to encourage plenty of flowers to form, and not to try to obtain fewer, larger blooms, for any overfeeding which encourages bigger flowers reduces their number and is inclined to cause ungainly growth. There is a wide colour range available, although many tints and tones found in the large flowered varieties cannot yet be had. Apart from the normal shaped flowers, considerable work has been done, particularly in the United States of America, in raising pendula begonias with attractive carnation, rose-bud, and camellia-shaped blooms.

This type of begonia is grown in exactly the same way as the other types. A point to remember is that certain varieties form only medium sized tubers, so that when buying in a stock some tubers may appear to be smaller. This is not an indication that they are inferior, but is simply typical. One can usually be sure that the medium sized tubers are young and therefore, are likely to be more vigorous than bigger older tubers. Even so, there are some older tubers which grow to a large size, and yet remain strong and free flowering for years.

Basket begonias are more sensitive to irregular supplies of moisture than the single and double sorts. Especially when the baskets are hung outdoors on the veranda or in the sun-porch, the compost may dry out fairly quickly, so that regular and thorough waterings are necessary. These waterings will certainly make the containers heavy, which means they must be fixed firmly so there is no likelihood of their falling down, especially in exposed or windy places where protection should be given.

To ensure the plants grow really bushy, any that do not branch out well while they are young, should have the tops of the stems nipped out. This causes plenty of side shoots to develop, resulting in bushiness.

Many specialists offer their own varieties, but the following can be depended upon as being showy, free flowering and reliable. Alice Manning, yellow; Blanche, white; Broad-acre, rich rose; Edith, salmon-pink; Flaming Torch, orange-scarlet; Golden Shower, a peach coloured camellia type; Rosina, rose pink; Scarlet Glow, fiery-scarlet; Shirley Desire, rosy-pink and Sunset, salmon-orange.

There are several varieties of the multiflora group which

make bushy plants, some of the growths of which are inclined to droop slightly. These however, are more suitable for summer bedding, where their loose growth is most effective.

Among the tuberous begonias, there are some small flowered sections, one of which is known as the multiflora group. As the name suggests, many flowers are produced, the smallness of the blooms being balanced by the great freedom with which they are carried.

Originating from the Andean species, B. Davisii, plants in

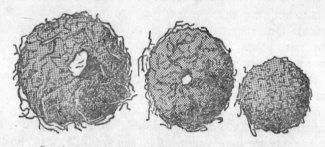

Sturdy begonia tubers. Multiflora varieties always produce smaller tubers.

this section are of dwarf bushy habit, which makes them ideal for summer bedding as well as being useful for growing in pots in the greenhouse. There are single, semi-double and a few double named sorts, although they are not all of good form, and there does appear to be a definite opening here for hybridists to work on the improvement of the present varieties and for the introduction of new sorts.

Some of the first crosses which produced the multiflora varieties were made well over eighty years ago and since that time several leading seedsmen have worked on improvements. This type of begonia will stand a considerable amount of sunshine which many of the larger types cannot bear. This may very well be because the abundance of their foliage does provide shade at the roots preventing them from drying out. General culture is the same as for ordinary large

flowered tuberous hybrids and the multifloras can be propagated vegetatively.

Seed is sometimes available although it does not usually
come true, and plants raised from seed have so far not
proved to be of much value. As to varieties, Flamboyant is
one of the very best and perhaps the most widely grown at
present. The single bright red flowers are most brilliant and
while the variety well lives up to its name, its colour does
not offend. Other good varieties which are likely to be obtainable, include, Alice Crousse, semi-double salmon-pink;
Count (or Graf) Zeppelin, semi-double vermilion-orange;
Madame Helene Harms, canary-yellow semi-double; Paul
Henri, bright red, double; Rambouillet, semi-double bright
red, with bronzy foliage; Santa Barbara, orange-vermilion,
with bronze tinted foliage; and Willem Eysser, a bright red,
double flowering sort with dark green leaves. With some
of these hybrids, the influence of species B. Davisii is
obvious.

There is another small section of tuberous rooted begonias, consisting of varieties carrying flowers of a pendulous
habit. Used and grown in the same way as the multiflora they
are known as B. bertinii hybrids. They were introduced by
a Frenchman M. Bertini which accounts for the name, and
it is usually reckoned that the first of these, which was known
as Begonia bertinii, and which produced long pointed rich
red flowers, came from the species B. boliviensis. Although
not widely known or grown, there are still bertinii hybrids in
cultivation, and of recent years some excellent new varieties
have been raised in the United States.

CHAPTER TEN

Cane Stemmed Sorts

ANOTHER VERY interesting group of fibrous rooted begonias, consists of the varieties having bamboo or cane-like stems. There are a number of species with this characteristic and these have been used to develop quite a large selection of varieties, many having in addition to their distinguishing stems, most attractively shaped and coloured foliage. Some will grow five or six feet high, although for general use they are usually divided long before they reach an awkward size.

The fact that the plants are kept in pots, will of course, restrict their root system which will keep them of reasonable size for a good many years.

Among the chief species of fibrous-rooted, cane-stemmed begonias are, B. coccinea with shiny green leaves and clusters of coral coloured flowers; B. albo-picta with smallish narrow glossy leaves on which are silver spots or small marks, and greenish-white flowers.

B. dichroa likes more warmth than most of this type. It is not of such pleasing habit of growth as the others in this section since it is inclined to be of a spreading or sprawling growth, although this is made very slowly. The flowers produced are of an attractive orange shade and no doubt if this colour could be reproduced in some hybrids of better habit than B. dichroa itself, it would be a great advance.

Other species in this section, but which are not often seen include B. aconitifolia with well divided leaves prominently marked silver-white. B. olbie is notable for its thick, well-lobed, bronzy-green, hairy leaves and white flowers. B. undulata is of rather spreading habit with reddish-pink

9. A well-furnished Begonia Greenhouse.

10. Double Ruffled Begonia.

11.   *Above*: Rose-form Double Picotee Flower.

12.   *Below*: Begonias at the Chelsea Flower Show.

13. Pendula Begonia—"Lou Anne."   *Photo by courtesy Blackmore & Langdon Ltd.*

14. Double Begonia—"Rhapsody."   *Photo by courtesy Blackmore & Langdon Ltd.*

15. Double Begonia—"Corona"—new 1966.   *Photo by courtesy Blackmore & Langdon Ltd.*

16. Gloxinia—The Duchess.

17. Double Multiflora.

stems and from it and other species have come a number of interesting hybrids.

Begonia corallina is somewhat similar to B. coccinea, and as far as the average amateur grower is concerned, it is its derivatives which are of importance and interest. Of these B. lucerna is especially noteworthy, for apart from its own great value, it has been instrumental in producing various hybrids, all of which have thick stems, large ever-green leaves and very freely produced flowers.

B. lucerna itself makes a really large plant, anything from five to seven feet high, and well over four feet in width. The attractive deep olive green stems, are very erect and rigid in the case of older plants, being as much as an inch thick. The oblique, rather leathery leaves are frequently ten inches or more in length and up to five or six inches wide. They are a rather dull, olive-green colour, greatly brightened by white spots or markings and a bronzy flushing, while the undersides are a reddish-purple.

The quite handsome flowers are produced in drooping clusters made up of several dozen individual flowers which are often one and a half inches long and an inch wide. Although sometimes both male and female flowers are found in the same truss, they are usually borne separately, the latter usually being a deeper colour and normally lasting longer than the male blooms. Begonia Lucerna is constantly in flower and is very showy for the living-room, conservatory and greenhouse.

It is a plant which will stand some amount of neglect and is not so likely to suffer as a result of irregular watering and draughts as are most begonias.

While not fastidious regarding soil, this decorative begonia and in fact all the cane stemmed sorts, do best in a mixture of three parts good fibrous loam, one part each of leaf mould, granulated peat and old cow manure, half part of coarse silver sand, with a three-inch potful of powdered charcoal and wood ash to each peck of the mixture. Really sharp drainage should be provided and firm potting carried out. Attention must be paid to the systematic stopping of the

c

leading growths so that really well shaped, bushy plants are secured.

It is not difficult to propagate cane stemmed begonias, and the tops of lateral growth will usually root readily if inserted in very sandy compost on the greenhouse bench, or in pans or boxes. If a propagating case or frame is available, it will result in the rapid production of well rooted young plants.

Although not cane-stemmed, there are other groups of fibrous rooted begonias worthy of mention, especially so since most of them have very attractive ornamental foliage. Some of these are species which have for long been known in cultivation, others are hybrids of real merit. One quite small species with finely divided foliage is B. foliosa. B. angularis has pointed greyish green leaves; B. cathayana is particularly beautiful although it requires a fairly high temperature. There are a number of named crosses from this species, some have the most delightfully marked foliage, which in certain cases, is covered with coloured hairs.

One particularly noteworthy variety is Velvet Queen, which has soft thick, velvet-like leaves of yellowish-green with prominent pinkish coloured hairs and a dark red under surface. It often produces quite attractive flesh pink flowers, although the leaves make it an ornamental plant of value. B. echmosepala is quite large growing, often attaining a height of three or four feet. The glossy green leaves have prominent dark veins, and apart from the pink flowers, the whole plant is quite decorative.

Begonia haageana comes from Brazil, and although there has for long been confusion regarding the name, it now seems pretty certain that the correct priority name should be B. scharffi. In some ways this is a pity, since there is another Brazilian begonia, which bears the name of Scharffiana, which means that confusion can easily arise due to the similarity of the names.

B. haageana (or Scharffi) is of fairly tall growing shrubby habit and likes warm or stove conditions. Its mid-green foliage is red underneath, and it has many soft white hairs.

The pale pink flowers are produced in clusters. The form known as B. haageana drostii seems to be a taller growing and appears to have a purplish shading on the undersides of the leaves.

B. scharffiana has rather fleshy, furry, dark green pointed leaves carried on prominent red stems. From it have come a number of really good named hybrids, all with ornamental foliage and clusters of flowers in shades of lighter pink or white.

B. sanguinea has shiny rich green, thick leaves shaded red on the undersides. This again has produced a number of really good hybrids, all of which have characteristic hairy leaves.

One of the very best in this section is B. metallica, which although old is still worth growing. The leaves are a dark or bronzy-green brightened by a metallic shine which combined with the dark veins and light hairs, makes the plant most noticeable. It has clusters of pretty pink flowers and has been much used in producing many first-class hybrids which are valued for their ornamental foliage and general decorative appearance.

The recently introduced hybrid Begonia, Silver Star coming from the United States, is a distinctive addition to the fibrous rooted, foliage class.

This hybrid, the result of crossing of B. caroliniaefolia and B. Lehmannii, shows the characteristics of both parents. The former is of Mexican origin and has a very erect stem and rhizomatous roots. The large leaves are made up of six or more fleshy toothed leaflets. B. Lehmannii is also of Mexican origin and has slender, rather creeping roots. The leaves in this case, consist of roundish lobes and are prettily marked with silver.

The appearance and habit of this plant is more or less between that of its two parents, making a fairly big stem, the leaves being well lobed and cut edged. The foliage is made more beautiful by a silvery sheen which seems to increase as the plant ages, while the undersides of the foliage have a purple tinge. The flowers appear during the spring and grow on stems twelve to fourteen inches high, being more or less star-shaped and of a clear white colour.

It is not difficult to cultivate, for it will grow in any good fibrous compost which is rich in humus matter. It is possible to pinch out the growing tips of any badly placed shoots. This helps to keep the plant shapely. Both stem and leaf cuttings may be secured in the spring, and if inserted in pans or boxes of light sandy compost, they will soon root, especially if provided with a warm, fairly close atmosphere.

CHAPTER ELEVEN

Propagation

THE EASIEST and quickest way to increase stock is by taking stem cuttings which can be secured from April until September. They can come either from the actual tubers or can be the side shoots on the main stems.

The best way of taking the cuttings, is to make a V or wedge shaped cut, that is to cut both sides of the stem with a sharp knife until the two cuts meet in a point. Cuttings taken from fairly low down on the stems, root much quicker and form better plants than those from towards the top of the growths, which are liable to be soft, sappy and to rot easily.

The endeavour should be to make the cuts so that the joint or edge at the base is not bruised or damaged in any way. Care is needed so that the stem from which the cutting is taken is not mutilated. Normally such cuts heal quite quickly. If they do not do so, they should be cleaned and dusted with yellow sulphur or some similar fungicide.

While not absolutely necessary the base of the cuttings can also be given a dusting of sulphur, the idea being to prevent mildew. It also helps in the quick formation of a callus and the production of roots. Should there be signs of mildew or rot appearing on the cuttings at soil level after they have been inserted, they should be taken out of the soil, cleaned, dusted with sulphur or Folosan, and replanted.

The cuttings can be easily bruised or broken and must be handled with care at all times. It will not do to push the cuttings into the soil mixture since the base might be damaged; it is wisest to first make a hole with a thin stick or even a pencil and then insert the cutting so that it is firmly held by a depth of up to an inch of soil.

A good rooting medium which is used by many amateur and professional raisers of begonias, consists of equal parts of good loam, peat or leaf mould and silver sand. Use small pots for each cutting for this makes it easier when the rooted cuttings need moving to larger receptacles.

Where space is limited however, the cuttings can be started in shallow trays or boxes, or a number can be inserted in large pots. It is a recognised fact that when cuttings of any kind are grown around the edge of the pots they usually root well. This is because there is less likelihood of the roots lacking moisture at any time, since they are able to make use of the water usually held by earthenware or clay pots.

After a light watering has been given, to make sure the compost is moist, the cuttings should be placed in the light but shaded from the direct rays of the sun. Ideally a propagating frame with a bottom heat of 65 degrees F. is the place to start the cuttings but since such a facility may not be available to everyone, other means must be employed. The planted receptacles can be stood in a deepish box and covered with glass which should be turned once or twice daily. It is important to avoid excessive dampness which could lead to damping off troubles.

To encourage a buoyant atmosphere, a little ventilation or air can be allowed. Close moist conditions encourage the cuttings to root well but continued damp stuffiness is bound to lead to trouble.

Wherever the cuttings are kept, care is needed to ensure that all the named sorts remain properly labelled. It is so easy to pull out a label, perhaps to stir the surface soil in the pot and then not return it to its place. It is also unwise to trust to one's memory when a batch of cuttings of different varieties is taken. This applies particularly where a number of sorts are being started in one box or tray.

Once the cuttings are well rooted, they can be grown on in the usual way, being moved to larger pots according to the development made. Where the cuttings are not taken before the middle of August and they are started singly in small pots. it is not necessary to pot them in the first season. for they will not have sufficient time to make a lot of growth the first season. In such cases only small tubers will have formed before the young plants take their winter rest. The following season, they and all others are started in the usual way.

Although it is chiefly the large flowered double and single tuberous begonias that are raised from cuttings, there are several other types and groups of which stock can be increased from stem cuttings. These include some of the fibrous and cane-stemmed varieties and the Hiemalis and Lorraine sorts. Regarding the latter two groups, the cuttings are best secured towards the end of the year, when suitable terminal growths are most likely to be available in the right condition. It is often possible to secure basal growths which will root with ease.

Begonia semperflorens can be propagated from basal cuttings secured as soon as the plants start into fresh growth after their resting period. Other species and types too, may be increased similarly. This saves time and avoids having to wait for the stems to develop before securing stem cuttings.

Although as previously mentioned, the compost must be moist when the cuttings are put in, it is permissible to give a light overhead sprinkling of water. This must not be overdone, in fact, it is preferable to keep the foliage on the dry side to discourage any possibility of rot or mildew gaining a hold.

Begonia cuttings can also be inserted during the summer using a sandy soil mixture under the cold frame. Keep the frame closed and if shade is given and the soil is nicely moist to begin with, little or no flagging will occur. After a month, the cuttings should be well rooted and can be potted up singly.

Many begonias including the winter flowering hiemalis, Lorraine and the Rex groups can also be propagated by leaf cuttings. This is very fortunate especially where few stem cuttings can be obtained. As would be expected, leaves take longer than stem cuttings to root and develop into nice plantlets.

Another way in which some tuberous and many rhizomatous begonias can be propagated is by division. This may not be an ideal way with tuberous begonias for undoubtedly stem cuttings are best. Sometimes however, when stock of a particular sort is extremely limited, it is well worth dividing. It may in fact, become necessary to do so to begin working up a stock.

The way to do this is to cut the tuber so that each piece contains a really good shoot or growing eye. If this is carefully done, it should not present any problems. After cutting it is advisable to well dust each cut portion with powdered charcoal or yellow sulphur. Since the cut surfaces will be moist this powder should easily adhere. Then the cut portions are planted in the same way as the ordinary tubers.

Propagation of the rhizomatous and various other types of begonias, including the popular Rex varieties, is slightly different, since these roots are not normally dried off as happens with the tuberous types. The best method is to take the roots out of the pots and then to remove the soil or as much as possible of it without damaging any of the roots. Make sure, of course, that any roots showing signs of decay are removed. Then separate the rhizomes so that each section has a strong healthy portion which can be potted up separately.

One usually finds even when it is not possible to be certain that each portion of rhizome has an eye on it, that it normally sprouts well. It is perhaps advisable to remove some of the older, bigger leaves when the roots are being divided, for this allows the rhizomes to start the job of producing fibrous roots more quickly without having to support much foliage. Once the divided roots have been potted or boxed, place them in a propagating frame or warm greenhouse to become established. Water with care and once the new plants are growing well, they can be treated in the ordinary way.

The easiest and perhaps the best way for gardeners to

obtain a stock of tuberous begonias is by raising the plants from seed. It is important to begin with really first-class seed, since this is no more difficult to grow than seeds of poor quality from an unknown origin. The seed is very fine, in fact, is one of the smallest known, which means that it needs special care in sowing. What appears to be a small quantity of seeds in a packet obtained from a leading seedsman, does in fact, contain many seeds, since they are so minute.

In the case of F.I. hybrids, these have to be obtained by hand pollination, which means that they are rather more expensive than the ordinary kinds, so that you will only get a small quantity in a packet, but even so, the number is usually sufficient for the average gardener.

Seed can be sown from January onwards, although it is a waste of time and seeds, to sow, if you cannot maintain a minimum temperature of 60 degrees F. If, of course, you have an electrically heated propagator, you will probably be able to keep a temperature of at least 70 degrees, but do not subject the seedlings to a very high temperature, and a dry atmosphere.

Seed sown in January, will normally produce really good flowering plants by the following summer. This can be considered quite remarkable, in view of the size of the plants produced, and the quantity of really large blooms which normally develop. Seeds can be sown in three-inch pots or pans, which should be filled with good compost.

The John Innes seed compost may be used, or it is quite easy to make up a simple mixture of equal parts of loam, peat and silver sand, all of which should be passed through a fine sieve. Peat is certainly a necessity, since its presence ensures that the compost does not dry out readily. In addition, when the seedlings are being pricked out they will be easier to transfer, because peat encourages plenty of fibrous roots, and it also makes it easier to life out the seedlings.

Some growers use vermiculite, since this has the quality of retaining moisture. This material however, does not contain any nutrient properties, so that the seedlings must be

c*

pricked out as soon as possible. Whatever type of container is used, it should first be lined with broken crocks and roughage, such as fibrous peat or leaf mould. The sowing medium should be well watered before use, and left to drain for some hours before sowing.

Never press the seed into the compost, and do not cover the sown receptacles with glass and paper, as is advised for some subjects. Once the seed has been sprinkled on the surface of the compost, the pot or pan should be placed in a propagator or other warm place. Since the seed is so tiny, and difficult to sow evenly, some growers mix it with fine silver sand. This greatly helps in ensuring that every seedling has plenty of room from its earliest stages. In addition, it lessens the possibility of damping off.

If the containers are plunged right up to their rims in peat, leaf mould or similar material, it will keep the compost from drying out, and be a great help in encouraging a good and even germination.

As a rule, germination occurs within ten days or so of sowing and it is frequently possible to start pricking out the seedlings fifteen to eighteen days later. Alternatively, one can wait until the third leaf, which is the first true leaf, has formed, since it is then rather easier to do the job. At this time the seedlings will be too delicate to handle separately, and they are usually planted out in little blocks, or ' patched out ' is the name professional growers give to this operation.

This job requires patience and for convenience a small pronged stick, such as is often supplied with fig boxes at Christmas, should be used for lifting the seedlings. Care must be taken to ensure that close contact is made between the soil holding the group of seedlings, and the soil in the tray or pot to which they are being transferred. Unless this is done, some of the seedlings may die, because of drying out. These small groups are usually placed about a quarter inch apart, and the same seed compost may be used. After being pricked out the plants are returned to warmth, a propagator being most useful.

Later, when the young plants are just touching each other

in the trays, they can be moved singly into small pots. Keep
the compost nicely moist, but not wet, and provide ventilation so that the plants grow into sturdy specimens. It is best
to water by standing the pots in vessels of shallow water, and
not by pouring water on the top.

Later still, the plants will have to be moved into bigger
pots according to growth made. The first flowers from a
January sowing will normally appear about the middle of
August. Throughout the whole of this period, the young
seedlings and plants should be kept growing vigorously and
moisture should remain available until the leaves discolour
and begin to fall off.

When this happens the soil can be knocked out of the pots
and the little tubers extracted and stored in a box of slightly
moistened peat or compost. They can remain in a dry frost-
proof place until early the following year when they can be
started in the usual way.

Stagnant air and overwatering causes damping off, so that
although sufficient moisture must always be available, ventilation must be regularly given. Moisture, air and light are
needed to produce and maintain compact, free flowering,
growth, which can be further aided by regular feeds of liquid
manure during the growing season.

CHAPTER TWELVE

Raising New Varieties

IN ALL of us there is a natural desire to create and for those who have the patience, the hybridising and the raising of new varieties of begonias, is a fascinating pastime. Sowing seed from any reliable source conjures up all sorts of possibilities concerning the resultant plants, for in sowing seeds of hybrid begonias, one can never be sure of what the new plants will produce.

If however, the seed to be sown has been obtained as a result of the grower himself having pollinated two flowers of his choice, the thrill of anticipation is greatly increased.

The chances that anything spectacular will be secured are slight but it is the possibility, that spurs on the hybridist. We must never assume that because we use two absolutely tip top varieties as parents, the resultant plants are bound to be winners. In many cases, the seedlings will revert and become similar to a primitive ancestor, which compared with present day varieties, is not worth anything. They may be of poor constitution or have some undesirable characteristic. Sometimes, too, a seedling will be so very like one of its parents, that it cannot be given a separate name, since it is not distinct. The perseverance of the plant breeder makes him the optimist he is, otherwise he would soon give up.

To avoid cluttering up the greenhouse with young plants of little merit, it is necesary to be ruthless and retain only the seedlings which show real merit and are different. Even in such cases, latent traits may develop making it necessary to destroy the plants.

It may very well be that many crosses will be made and no worth-while new plant secured. The moment of joy comes when one realises that they have something which is really different and of value.

We must begin with an object in mind, for if we are going to cross pollinate haphazardly, we might just as well leave the matter to nature herself who has not really served us badly, seeing the many natural hybrids which have come to us.

While it is not essential for the hybridist to know the laws of cytology, he should seek some information regarding the make-up of a flower and have just a little information on plant cells and their development.

Some knowledge of the mendel theory will also help in knowing what to expect and what to breed for, especially if the hybridist intends to continue with the work for some years. It is a good plan to do this, for one cannot expect to know everything about plant breeding or to obtain full results in one or two years.

Mendelism is a term used to commemorate Gregor Mendel the Austro-Silesian monk, who lived from 1822 until 1884, and who carried out a number of breeding experiments, the results of which have been of tremendous help to plant breeders. It was from his work that the dominant and recessive factors in breeding, were recognised. The outstanding example we have from Mendel is in garden peas. He found that by crossing a tall variety with a dwarf sort, the result in the first year was all tall growing plants. This tallness, Mendel termed as dominant factor. In the next generation, seeds from the tall plants showed a quarter of the group as true and tall, half were tall but untrue, or unfixed, and the remaining quarter were dwarf, and fixed, and this continued to be so in successive generations.

It is of course, essential to start with the right varieties, and those which have the characteristics we wish to produce or emphasise, in addition to those already possessed. We therefore, select one flower as the female or seed bearing parent, and one as the male parent from which the pollen will be obtained. To the naked eye, pollen is just like coloured dust, each grain being a minute speck, although it does vary in colour, size and shape. It is one of the miracles of nature that such very tiny grains contain the living germ and such energy and power, resulting under the right conditions, in life development.

It will be, a good plan to consider very briefly the process of fertilisation. The female part of the flower is the pistil at the top of which is the stigma, which actually crowns the part known as the style. It is on the stigma that the pollen must fall, or be placed if fertilisation it to be effected. It is able to hold the pollen, since at the right stage, it is slightly sticky and in a very short time the pollen grain grows and sends out a protrusion or tube. This forces its way into the stigma through the cells of the style, and enters the ovary in which is an embryo sac, where it ultimately unites with the female gamete or cell. The result is, the formation of an embryo plant with potential root, stem and leaves. The whole process is very rapid and may be completed within a few hours. It will be readily understood that subsequent good culture cannot make a first-class healthy plant from seed, which has been developed from inferior or unhealthy plants.

The male parts of the flower are the anthers, or little pollen sacs at the top of the stamens, which when they are ripe will burst and distribute the pollen. In the normal way, this pollen falls on the stigma of the same flower. This of course, is self pollination, but when the pollen is transferred from one flower to another, either by insects, wind or through human agencies, this is said to be cross pollination.

To safeguard the stigma of the flower, which is to be the female parent, it is wise to carefully remove the anthers while they are very young, and before pollen develops. With care, it can be done without harm to the rest of the bloom, for the anthers can be lifted out by the use of forceps or cut off with scissors. Such action will prevent the possibility of the selected flower being accidentally self-pollinated.

The operation of transferring pollen to the female flower, although not difficult, must be done with the greatest of care, since the reproductive organs of the flowers, are most delicate. It is quite usual to transfer the pollen by using a camel-hair brush. Perhaps the easiest way is to pick off the male or pollen bearing flower, and either dust the pollen on to the stigma of the female bloom, or to bring it lightly into direct contact with the stigma when some of the pollen will adhere and subsequently lead to fertilisation and the setting of seed.

Water by immersion, letting moisture seep
through drainage hole

Normally, the majority of double flowering begonias produce extremely little pollen, and this is one main difficulty when trying to raise new varieties by hybridisation. Consequently, it is necessary to take steps to ensure that more pollen is produced. Experience has proved that if the selected plants are treated well, and grown so that they make good bushy specimens which produce many flowers, they are more likely to yield the required pollen. Fully double flowers will not do so, therefore, the plants must be induced to produce flowers which are pollen-bearing although it is not wise using the pollen on all semi-double and single flowers which usually produce pollen freely, and one must keep up the percentage of double seedlings produced by constructive action.

In the case of doubles, if the plants have been flowering freely for some time, any feeding should be lessened or stopped altogether, and water applied less liberally. Semi-double flowers will then appear from the same stems, and pollen can be secured from the flowers on these side shoots. It may confidently be assumed that this pollen will pass on the quality of doubleness to its offspring.

The flowers selected as the female or seed bearer, should be of proper shape and of the right quality from a good growing plant. After it is obvious that the cross has taken, which will be evident by the swelling of the little seed pod which is behind the petals, any remaining flowers on the stem should be removed, so that the developing seeds are encouraged to grow.

While a warm congenial atmosphere is needed for effective fertilisation, it should not be too dry, although really damp conditions too, must be avoided. The natural tackiness of the stigma when it is at the receptive stage, will ensure the pollen being retained, and lead to proper fertilisation.

Every care must be taken to prevent the selected female flower, being pollinated by insects or other means, before one has time to make the desired cross. The chosen blooms can be protected by little polythene bags or even covered with tissue paper, which may be retained for a day or two, after the cross has been made.

It is always a matter of great interest and help to keep a proper record of the crosses made, and results obtained, for not only does this show which varieties have produced the best offspring, but it indicates too, those which are unsuitable as parents because they bring out weaknesses, or undesirable traits.

Most raisers label both the plants, and keep a separate record, which becomes a permanent means of checking work done in previous years. If against each cross made, the year is also indicated, it will be of help when later, previous records are referred to.

Once the petals have fallen, the little seed pod will swell fairly quickly, and normally after from six to eight weeks from the time the pollinating was carried out, the seed will be ready for harvesting. The pods must be gathered before they split open, otherwise the seed will be lost. It is rather lightish brown seed which is usually the most viable, very dark, almost black seed is often sterile, because of an ineffective cross, or some incompatibility. This is why sometimes although apparently good seed has been sown under ideal conditions, there is no sign of growth.

Great as has been the advance in begonia breeding during the last few decades, there is still room for fresh development and as with other flowers, perseverance brings its reward. I am not sure that we need a blue begonia, but we do want scent, and a wider colour range in some sections, and also more which produce strong sturdy stems, which are able to firmly hold double flowers however heavy they may be. The possibilities are great, and one can be certain that begonia breeders are no less conscious of the needs than are raisers of other types of flowers.

CHAPTER THIRTEEN

Exhibiting Begonias

ANYONE WHO has seen the marvellous displays of begonias set up by some of the trade growers at horticultural shows may feel that it is impossible for the average amateur gardener to attain such results. At the same time, one may well be inspired to grow begonias for exhibition purposes. Certainly with careful and continued attention, it is possible for the small grower with an average sized greenhouse, to raise some really first-class plants which will be capable of creating a favourable display on the show bench.

When shown in a class calling for any flowering pot plant, a well grown begonia will always command the judges' interest. It is, however, in the classes where begonias are specifically asked for, that such almost dazzling displays are sometimes seen. The family is so large that it is not at all unusual for there to be separate classes for the tuberous rooted, fibrous-rooted, foliage and species groups, so that there is an opportunity for exhibiting a wide range of plants.

The initial cultivation of tuberous begonias for show purposes is the same as for plants for general decoration. Although February is not too soon to box or pot up the tubers there is no advantage in starting then, unless a fairly even temperature, preferably not less than 50 to 55 degrees F.; can be maintained. Somewhat higher will be a help but fluctuations must be avoided.

Low temperatures, particularly at night, increase the chance of the corms rotting. It is unnecessary, in fact unwise, to add artificial fertiliser to the soil mixture used for starting the tubers. A good root system is needed before a lot of top growth is made. Avoid over watering, but do not let the soil dry out.

Having carefully grown the plants in the way indicated in the chapter on cultivation, make sure that only the finest, healthiest plants are reserved for showing. Regular examination of the tubers should be made, so that the soundness of the plant may be maintained.

Where individual pot plants are being entered in a particular class, there will be no need for action in providing staging material. Where a group of plants is being staged, one can assume that the appropriate tiered staging will be provided. It is advisable to take some suitable black material for use as a background. This cloth, fixed on to the tiered staging, not only covers the unsightliness of the wooden benches, but shows up the colour of the flowers to advantage. Nowadays it is not unusual for green, grey or maroon material to be used. These are suitable so long as they fit in with the colours of the blooms being shown. On the whole, black is safer, since it shows off the colour tones to advantage.

It is not really difficult to pack plants to take to a local show, although it must be said here, that if the plants are brought uncovered out of a warm house, they may easily be spoiled by the effects of sudden exposure to a lower temperature or by cutting winds.

The result will be either that the flowers will droop or fall right off or the petals will become badly marked. This sometimes happens some hours after the exposure of the blooms and may not be evident until after the plants have been staged. The remedy is obvious. Cover the entire plant with tissue paper or some similar light material every time they are moved into a lower temperature while being transported to the show.

Having selected the appropriate plants for exhibiting, it is then important to ensure that the flowers are at their best by the show date. This means care and consideration. A certain amount of ' stopping ' will have to be done. The reduction in the number of shoots with the consequent smaller number of flowers allowed, means that the available food and strength go to the production of top quality blooms.

These flowers will be larger and of a finer quality than they would be if all blooms had been allowed to develop, although once these exhibition flowers are over, there will be no successional display.

As a guide, it may be reckoned that it takes a month for a bud when first seen, to develop into a full sized, open flower suitable for the exhibition table.

One of the main difficulties concerning the exhibiting of begonias arises from the necessary packing of plants and transporting them to the show. Sometimes there are classes for begonias as cut flowers. In these cases, the flowers are cut with a good stem and placed in a shallow vessel of water for some hours to help them fill out.

They should then be handled carefully and packed flat in a well lined box, placing the blooms so that they are kept in position by the tissue paper and cotton wool used. The flowers are shown either in separate vases or in tubes fitted to boards, the latter usually being supplied by the Society demanding this method of exhibiting. The show schedule will of course, give details as to what is required in this direction.

The greatest care is needed when taking or sending pot plants to a show. As far as the fibrous and rhizomatous varieties are concerned, it is normally sufficient to see that the plants are well staked, and that no stem is likely to be bruised or fall outside the supports which have been applied. Precautions must be taken to ensure that the stems do not rub against any supporting stick or tie made. Make sure too, that the flowers are not exposed to winds at any stage, for it is easy for the petals to become bruised or torn.

The double tuberous varieties are a different matter, for the weight of the flower head alone, will make it easy for the stems to snap off. Each stem must be firmly fixed to a cane, not too tightly, but so as to prevent any possibility of it moving or being jolted in transit. Some growers and exhibitors find it best to use wire supports which need to be covered with some soft material to prevent chafing. The wires are inserted into the pot or in some cases, fit on to the pot themselves. They are made so that the blooms actually rest on the top of the supports, although the utmost care is needed when lifting the flowers to rest them in position, for the heads will easily snap off. Such supports prevent any jogging and bruising in transit.

There are various other means and it is usually possible for the exhibitor to contrive his own method of conveyance. It is surprising what can be done when there is interest and where some effort is made.

As a general guide to exhibitors, the following information is extracted (by permission of the Royal Horticultural Society) from the Horticultural Show Handbook. This indicates what judges are looking for.

Meritorious. A well-balanced plant, bearing flowers in size and number proportionate to the size of the plant. Large flowers of good substance, circular in outline, with broad overlapping petals, culminating in one centre. Colour decided and clear. Foliage which is clean, healthy and undamaged. Stems which are stout and erect.

Defective. An ill-balanced plant, carrying flowers which are few or small for the size of the plant. Small flowers, of poor texture or irregular outline, or having decided centres. Long, narrow petals. Undecided or muddy colour. Pale or damaged or spotted foliage. Spindly weak stems.

The points system is worked out as follows: Plant – 4, Stems – 3, Form of flower – 6, Colour – 4 and Foliage – 3. Making a total of twenty points.

Although these requirements may appear to be severe and on a first reading of them it may seem to the grower of just a few begonia plants, that he will never have any specimens likely to fit in with requirements, in actual practice, it is not so difficult to grow good plants for the exhibition table. Perfection is unlikely to be attained but it is a good standard at which to aim!

If all exhibitors waited until they had perfect plants or

flowers, there would not be any flower shows at all.

Although a certain amount of extra attention is needed in bringing begonia plants to exhibition standards the required method of growing does present a challenge which keen growers will welcome. Generally speaking, the aim should be to secure really sturdy free flowering plants, in seven or eight-inch pots, although often plants in five-inch pots are very suitable for showing purposes.

When the plants are established in their final pots, it is a good plan to feed them every ten to twelve days with a liquid fertiliser having a high potash content, but used at weak strength. If all flower buds are removed until about six or seven weeks before the show date, it will ensure, that under ordinary conditions, flowers will be available when required.

Obviously the rate of growth largely depends on growing conditions and also on varieties. Tests have shown that a bud about an inch in diameter will usually produce a fully opened flower about five weeks later, although of course, under cool conditions it will be a day or two longer.

As the flower stem develops, it will usually be seen that it carries three buds. The two side buds should be pinched out and the large central one retained. Take special care not to touch the petals of the retained bud, otherwise they may show marks when the flower has opened.

Specialist exhibitors pinch out the growing point of both main and side shoots three or four weeks before the show date. As the blooms open, the top leaves should be moved away from the edges of the petals to prevent damaging or marking them in any way. If the leaves are badly placed, they may have to be removed altogether.

Some show schedules have a class for cut blooms. If you are entering such a class do not gather the flowers until a few hours before they are to be judged. Many show tents or rooms are very hot. In such an atmosphere the flowers may collapse within a short while. If it is necessary to cut some time before the show, which is quite likely, if the exhibition is at a distant place, the base of each flower stem should be wrapped in moist cotton wool, which should be fixed on to the stem with rubber bands or a raffia tie.

When exhibiting a group of begonia plants in pots some thought should be given to arrangement. Although tiered staging is usually provided by the show authorities but in any case, it is always best to break up the contour. If the central pots at the back of the exhibit are raised, it will give a better overall effect. When there is a choice of plants, the best specimens should be grouped in the centre. In doing so, make sure that each plant is fully seen to advantage and that one does not hide another. Never crowd an exhibit for if each plant is given plenty of space, their full value will be seen and appreciated.

Unless the schedule definitely says that no foliage or other plants are to be used in the begonia group, it will be permissible to include some suitable foliage subjects. One of the easiest to grow and one which fits in well with begonias, is Grevillea robusta, sometimes known as the Silky Oak. The narrow, finely cut foliage is most attractive, particularly when the plants are fairly young.

These plants can be raised from seed without difficulty. Then, of course, there is the asparagus fern and maidenhair fern. It is possible to stage a group consisting only of begonias, since there are a number of ornamental leaved species both green and colourful, which fit in well.

Before leaving the staged group look over each plant and remove any damaged or discoloured leaves making sure that each plant is placed to advantage. In the case of the tuberous begonias make sure the colours are nicely blended. It is an advantage for each plant to be clearly named, although all labels should be inconspicuous.

Many different kinds of begonias are used for exhibition but it is usually the large flowered doubles that are grown for this purpose. It is important to grow the plants well for their own sake, and to ensure that they flower when required, timing is important. It is useless having a plant in tip-top condition just before or just after a show, for undoubtedly judges will take freshness into consideration which means that timing is vital.

If selected plants show signs of coming into bloom well before the required time, the earliest buds can be removed and the latter set depended upon. This is one of the advantages in starting tubers early, since in any case, it is always easier to delay flowering than to bring it forward. The main flower show period is from mid-July to mid-September, and this means that it is advisable to start tubers between February and the second week in April.

As a guide, one may reckon that it will take about six weeks for a bud about the size of a shilling, to reach its best condition. This means that plants required for showing, should have their flower buds removed until six weeks before the show date. Selection of varieties plays an important part and it is wise to remember that the rich reds and very deep colours do not hold their blooms in good condition quite as long as the paler colour tones.

Strong plants are often inclined to produce more than one stem and care is needed in this connection since obviously, if more than one stem is allowed, the flowers produced will be smaller. In the case of extra strong growers, the flowers sometimes produce two centres. Any variety known to do this, is best grown as a two stemmed plant. It is definitely unwise to allow more than two stems excepting in the case of exceptionally strong plants, or those which are inclined to be coarse growing. In any event such varieties are unlikely to be very suitable for exhibition.

Obviously, the show schedule will decide the way in which begonias are to be staged but in some exhibitions, begonia flowers may be cut from the plants and exhibited on boards. If this is the plan, it is usually decided to allow each plant to produce one flower. To ensure this develops into a really large flower which is necessary for cut bloom show classes, a certain amount of foliage must be carefully removed.

This requires much care so that decay does not set in, and it will be helpful if whenever leaf or flower stems are pinched out, that the part from which it has been removed, is lightly dusted with yellow sulphur powder. Obviously, when only one flower per plant is allowed, timing is slightly more difficult and individual plants from which the single bloom is secured have little further decorative value for that season.

CHAPTER FOURTEEN

Pests, Diseases and Disorders

GROWN UNDER good conditions and looked after without being unduly fussed over, the begonia is comparatively free from ills and not likely to be the target of many pests or diseases. Even so, it is prudent of the grower to discover how to identify them and to know what to do to stop the increase of such troubles. So often they can be eradicated quickly if dealt with at once, whereas if they gain a hold, considerable effort may be required to put matters right.

It follows, that where various other plants are grown in the same greenhouse as begonias, that they too, must be kept in a clean condition. There are a number of fumigant smokes available and used in accordance with instructions, they are both safe and effective. Perhaps the most troublesome pest on begonias is red mite or red spider, which is liable to occur where there is a continued dry atmosphere. The tiny insect although invisible to the naked eye, can, if it gains a hold, cause a considerable amount of harm. It makes the leaves and sometimes the petals, distorted and curled, while in bad cases, it will even prevent the flower buds from developing. Should there be signs of the leaves becoming wrinkled they should be examined and if distinct reddish-brown strains are seen it is possible that the mite is there. Nicotine wash is an effective remedy so long as all of the foliage and stems are wetted.

Easier to obtain and very effective however, is Volck which is encouraged by a dry atmosphere. This will cause streaky markings on the leaves, which in bad cases, become brittle and break easily. Fumigant smokes, have proved effective in getting rid of thrips as they have against various types of aphis, although it is often easier to use an insecticide for the latter.

Root-knot eelworm will occasionally attack begonias and where it does occur, it is best to burn the plants. This pest causes swellings on both the roots and tubers. Remove all rubbish and decaying matter from around the plants and in fact, from the entire greenhouse, so that there is no possibility of the eelworm finding a resting place. Keep the soil in the pots sweet and avoid overwatering. Should there ever be an attack it is wise to work in some powdered naphthalene into the soil. Some growers use sterilised compost.

Cyclamen mite is rather uncommon and confined usually to greenhouses, where various types of plants are grown. It shows first as rusty brown stains on the foliage and stems the buds turning brown while young and falling off. It can be dealt with in the same way as recommended for red spider.

Dropping of buds and flowers

Several factors are responsible for this phenomenon, the foremost of which is high temperatures. Begonias are native to high altitudes in the tropics, growing from an elevation of five thousand feet up. This means cool daily temperatures and decidedly cool nights. In districts where the temperature becomes really high, buds and flowers will often drop off, but will hold in the autumn when nights are cooler.

Another factor is a poor root system. When plants are freshly transplanted, they will often drop their buds and flowers until they develop a new root system.

Plants that suffer from poor drainage and are heavily overwatered will often drop their buds completely. The soil should always be moist but never soggy. On the other hand extreme drying out and too sunny a situation will cause the same difficulty, too many leaves and not enough flowers.

Some begonias inherit a strong branching habit, and if several shoots are left on a tuber, especially if it is well fed, will form a very bushy plant with too much foliage. The flowers won't be able to come through. One can remove some of the upper leaves covering the lower shoots to let light in, but care should be taken to cut only the leaves, and to leave the leaf stems on the plant to mature and eventually fall off. If cut close to the main stem they may become diseased, infecting the main stem and destroying the plant.

To prevent extensive bushy growth, one should leave only one shoot per tuber, or if a large tuber, two or three shoots facing opposite directions, breaking off the remaining young shoots before they reach a height of two or three inches. The wounds should be left exposed to the air, and not covered for several days, in order to heal. It could also be done before the sprouting tubers are planted. Use a thumb or cut them off with a sharp knife, leaving only the strongest to grow.

Leggy plants with sparse bloom

The amount of light begonias receive governs their growth. If exposed to too much sunshine, they will be dwarf, forming thick shiny leaves and the flowers will burn. Extreme shade again produces very tall skinny plants with a few or no flowers at all. One should seek the happy medium where the plants get full light without direct sunshine, in which they will bloom profusely and will not grow too tall. In poor light they will simply grow leggy and not bloom.

Overfeeding

Begonias require judicious feeding in order to produce large, well formed, specimens, but overfeeding causes perhaps more damage and shortens their lives more than any other factor. The quick acting fertilisers such as fish meal and fish-emulsion are of organic nature and can hardly do damage unless used in excessive quantities.

The first sign of overfeeding is a rich bluish-green colour of the leaves, which curl under. The plants will produce distorted flowers smaller in size, but gradually as the nitrogen in the soil diminishes, they will come out of it and perform normally. If nitrogen is used in such forms as nitrate of soda, sulphate of ammonia or nitrate of potash, the plants will simply burn up if overfed. The growth will be stunted with small flowers or none, and upon maturing the tubers, you will find them completely hard.

The ideal feeding is to keep the plants always slightly hungry by giving them light doses of liquid fertiliser recommended for tuberous begonias, following the directions prescribed on the containers. If foliage is a blue-green withhold feeding as they are receiving too much nitrogen. Start feeding again when the foliage is a soft green colour. Very pale foliage is a sign of nitrogen deficiency and the need for increased feeding. The finest flowers form when plants are slightly underfed and the foliage is deep green.

Rotting of plants

The tissue of begonia plants is quite sensitive to any decaying material which they contact. If young plants are set out in a soil heavily enriched with manure and the decaying parts of the manure come in contact with the stem, the plant will often rot off at the base. This happens more in warmer conditions especially with high humidity.

A little clean soil or fine sand placed around the stem when planting seedlings will prevent the rotting off to a great extent. When flowering, the plants should be kept clean of all the debris of the old flowers and flower stems. Flowers should be removed leaving all of the flower stem or if cut, as much of the stem as possible, as the open wound immediately starts moulding. If a stem is left long enough, it will mature and fall off from the main stem before the mould can reach its entire length. If cut too short, the soil will infect the main stem and if not checked, will decay the whole plant eventually.

Old petals falling in the axil of the leaves may start mould, in an area which could be scraped clean with a knife, dried with a cloth, and dusted over with charcoal so it can heal. If the main stem is badly moulded, it can be cut off below the infected part or be completely removed if necessary. The plant should be kept slightly drier as it will send new shoots out as a rule trying to recover its health.

In this way tubers can be saved and although weakened, they may perform well again the following year. If stem rot is not checked, it will go all the way down into the tuber and destroy it completely.

Bacterial leaf-spot first appeared several years ago and attacks the plants chiefly in greenhouses where there is high humidity and not enough aeration. It is most damaging to the young seedlings in their germinating stage. It seldom attacks plants when they are larger and hardly ever if they are grown outdoors.

The latest and perhaps the most serious enemy is a new variety of mildew reported for the first time in 1951 in isolated areas. It has become widely spread ever since. Of all materials we have been gradually testing, spraying with Mildont as soon as first signs of it appears, will control it perfectly. If not controlled it will spread rapidly and destroy the appearance of the plants for the season. However the tubers should not be thrown away as they may grow perfectly the following season, since no disease is transmitted on them. Keeping the foliage dry especially at night also prevents the spread of any fungus disease.

Very rarely a virus infection will put in an appearance causing poor, stunted growth. Often affected plants will grow out of it; if they do not, they are best destroyed.

As far as actual diseases are concerned, the begonia is remarkably free from them. When they do occur it is usually possible to trace their origin and take steps to prevent further trouble. Although begonias like congenial conditions, they also like fresh air and when they have it there is much less likelihood of disease.

Stem rot will sometimes develop and is first seen as a small brown mark or patch on the main stem. If left this increases in size and may eat right through the stems. A whitish mould sometimes appears over the affected part.

If the disease is noticed early enough, the attacked portion can be carefully cut out and the stem will go on growing.

Otherwise, it should be cut right down in the hope that fresh growth will arise from the tubers.

After cutting any stems, it is wise to dust them with yellow sulphur or folosan, which greatly helps in the cleansing and healing process.

Overfeeding predisposes the plants to stem rot, and it is best to avoid artificial fertilisers and anything rich in nitrogen since these lead to soft growth.

Damping off of shoots and leaves is sometimes caused by faulty watering. If moisture is applied without care and there is a stuffy atmosphere, there is always a chance of fungus gaining a hold.

Leaves or buds which fall, should be removed, for if they remain lodging on the plants they may set up disease.

CHAPTER FIFTEEN

Introducing the Gloxinia

THE GLOXINIA is named after B. P. Gloxin a botanist of Colmar. The earliest history of this plant seems to be non-existent. It was about the year 1785 that the first record appeared and it was then named in honour of Gloxin. It does not seem to have been introduced into England until more than thirty years later, when it came from Brazil and was known as Gloxinia speciosa. It became popular fairly quickly and was soon to be found in important plant collections.

As mentioned by Weathers in his Bulb Book, 'it would be difficult to recognise this early plant as the parent of the present day gloxinia, with its large almost erect, regular blooms in innumerable shades and spottings.' The description of this first plant was given as follows: short stemmed, more or less hairy, with blunt or slightly pointed, oblong leaves. More or less convex, usually narrowed towards the base, crenulate on the margins, velvety in texture and sparsely clothed with hairs. Flowers with ovate, lance-shaped, velvety calyx segments; corolla tubular, bell-shaped, irregular, drooping, five lobed and usually violet in colour.

The modern gloxinia is now available in almost all shades of colour, excepting yellow and true blue. The colours range from white to crimson, and there are fiery reds, passing through purple to pale and deep violet, with pink in numerous shades. Apart from the self or uniform colours, there are many forms which are beautifully marked and spotted, these markings being quite different from the ground work colour. By raising seedlings there is always the possibility of unusual colour combinations appearing. This is what

18. Specimen Double Begonia Bloom.

19. Gloxinia, Royal Purple.

20. Roseform Picotee.

21. A Fine Double
Begonia—pot grown.

22. Double Begonia—"Alan Melville"—new 1966.

Photo by courtesy Blackmore & Langdon Ltd.

23. Gloxinia Panzer Beauty.

24. Saint Paulia, Single Pink Hybrid.

25. Roseform Wide Picotee.

26. *Below*: Ruffled Picotee.

makes plants such as gloxinias so interesting to raise from seed.

As has happened with other plants, botanists subsequently discovered that the gloxinia has been misnamed. They found that it belonged to the genus sinningia, so that correctly it should be Sinningia speciosa. This was described by early writers as having small neat purple-blue flowers. Because of the shape of the flower tube or corolla, of the earliest varieties, gloxinias are sometimes known as slipper blossoms. These 'slippers' had trumpets of about one and a half inches in diameter. When it is realised that many of the modern hybrids carry blossom anything from four and a half to six inches in diameter, the difference in size will be appreciated.

It was not long before British horticulturists saw the possibilities in using Gloxinia (or Sinningia) speciosa, in a breeding venture. It was this plant and Sinningia guttata with its spotted trumpets that have been chiefly responsible for many of the various coloured and mottled sorts in cultivation today.

While some commercial growers may be able to devote a greenhouse to the growing of one type of plant most of us have to cultivate a variety of subjects in the same structure. It is not usually possible or even desirable for the amateur gardener to give over the whole greenhouse to gloxinias. Fortunately these plants will stand very similar conditions to those required by a number of subjects especially the begonia. Both can be raised from seed and produce corms of similar appearance. Seed of both can be sown at the same time of year under identical conditions. It is after germination that difference is only in detail.

One of the main differences between gloxinias and begonias is in their root system. Those of gloxinias are very thin and like fine cotton, while in the case of begonias the roots, while by no means fleshy, are in comparison quite thick. This difference in roots gives a clear clue to the kind of soil most appreciated. Begonias like one of a moderately coarse texture while gloxinias with their delicate root system,

D

need a much more finely divided mixture. This means that the soil ingredients should be passed through a finer sieve than that needed for begonias. Fairly coarse grit can be added to the begonia compost but fine silver sand is best for gloxinias.

Another important difference between these plants is that

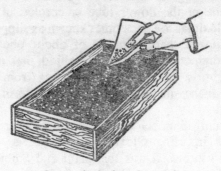

One method of sowing seed

whereas gloxinias like slightly acid conditions, which means that lime should be omitted, begonias prefer a sweet soil.

The least costly way of raising both items is from seed, although for larger plants with plenty of flowers the first season, it is better to obtain one year corms. First year seedling plants do not carry many flowers the first year and there are rarely more than six or seven blooms open at the same time which means that they are usually grown in five-inch pots. One year plants however, will flower most freely and may have several dozen blooms open at the same time. If the earliest batch of gloxinia corms is started into growth early in the year they will usually come into flower before the end of May. Seed sown in early January will not usually produce blooms before the middle of August.

Since both seeds and corms require the same temperature, which should not really be less than 65 degrees F. it does mean that providing the right heat in January is fairly costly, unless other subjects are being grown in the same house. Corms can, of course, be started in March when it will not be necessary to provide quite so much artificial heat.

Gloxinias like a moist atmosphere and this is particularly needed during the summer months when the greenhouse or even the living-room, can become hot and dry. A slightly shaded position is suitable and with a moist atmosphere, this does give the warmth and humidity in which plants flourish. To achieve these conditions frequent overhead sprayings with water in warm weather should be given but not, of course, applied when conditions are cooler or once the flowers are over. In a mixed house, to provide the slightly more shaded conditions needed by gloxinias, extra coatings of glasshouse shading such as Summer Cloud can be applied.

Generally speaking, gloxinias are not so long lived as begonias. There are known instances where begonias will go on flowering for eight or nine years although very often by that time, the corms have become rather unsightly and corky. It is rarely worthwhile keeping gloxinias for more than four years and the display is never quite so good as that given by the one year tuber.

There is no doubt that quality counts with gloxinias and no amount of expert attention will make a low grade specimen produce really first-class plants with the best quality blooms. It is therefore advisable to buy the best possible stock, for the extra cost will be well repaid.

When applying liquid or solid feeds do not overdo the nitrogen for although gloxinias do need this, too much leads to soft growth with excessive foliage. While gloxinias are sometimes said to be difficult subjects, with ordinary good care, such as can be given by the average gardener, their culture while presenting a challenge to the keen gardener is certainly within the ability of all. There is no doubt that once one begins cultivating gloxinias the desire to do so increases as success is achieved.

Both gloxinias and saintpaulias belong to the natural order or botanical family known as the gesneriacea. This family takes in many subjects all of which have the following general characteristics. The leaves are usually opposite, being fleshy, wrinkled and without stiples. The irregularly shaped flowers are sometimes produced in racemes or panicles, on other occasions they are solitary. The corolla is generally tubular or broadly bell-shaped, usually consisting of five lobes.

Among the other interesting members of this family are the achimenes, of which there are many fine hybrids. They make excellent subjects for pots and baskets. Whereas

Standing the seed tray in shallow water

gloxinias are grown from tubers, achimenes are propagated from tubercles, which are small, scaly rhizomes. They make excellent flowering plants throughout the summer. After the foliage has died down the tubercles can be left in the soil and stored in a dry place during the winter, where the temperature does not fall below 50 degrees F.

The columnea is another plant in the same family; most excellent for growing in baskets in the greenhouse. Flowering during the summer, it is most showy. It can be raised from cuttings of half-ripe wood, these being made into two or three-inch lengths and stripped of most of their leaves, and inserted in a pot of sandy compost in a warm propagating frame. Columnea banksii has particularly showy, bright orange flowers.

The gesnerias are also wonderfully showy subjects for the greenhouse. In recent years some of the hybrids have become known as Smithianthas. They are fine pot plants with erect spikes of tubular flowers carried above the ornamental foliage. They can be propagated from leaf cuttings in the same way as gloxinias.

Closely related to the achimenes and gesnerias is the isoloma. This is raised from scaly or catkin-like rhizomes and may be grown in exactly the same way as the achimenes.

Lastly we must mention the streptocarpus. These produce flowers in many charming colours often with attractive contrasting pencilled markings. They can be propagated by means of leaf cuttings or from seed. During the winter a temperature of 45 to 50 degrees F. is sufficient so long as the plants are kept on the dry side.

Other good, but little known, gesneriads which will grow well in a fairly rich well drained soil include the following. Aeschynanthus, which has trailing or climbing varieties, most suitable for hanging baskets. They have colourful leaves, which are beautifully veined and marked red on the undersides.

Among the interesting species are A. javanicus which has scarlet buds not unlike a ladies lipstick, which accounts for the common name of ' lipstick ' plant.

Allopelctus comes from Central and Southern America. Among the species are A. schlimii which is a handsome plant easily propagated from tip cuttings. The golden-yellow flowers have attractive red lines.

Chirita chinensis has beautiful silvery variegated leaves and thimble-like flowers of rich violet colour, well set off by the prominent yellow anthers.

Rechsteineria leucotricha is a tuberous rooted plant not often seen. It has silverish-white, hairy leaves and stems, the tubular flowers of salmon-red also being well covered with silvery hairs. Some of these gesneriads are difficult to find outside botanical gardens but they never fail to create interest when seen.

CHAPTER SIXTEEN

Cultivation

IT IS usual to start a collection of gloxinias by buying plants or tubers. It is only after one has grown plants for the first time that they become really enthusiastic about them. Sometimes, however, when plants in bud are purchased, they give disappointment.

This may very well be because the plants have been kept in a greenhouse, heated to a certain temperature, and when they are transferred to a shop or the buyer's living-room, conditions are often so very different and the buds fail to open and fall off before showing colour. A close, dry atmosphere will also cause buds to drop.

To do well, gloxinias need air, humidity, and the change from a moist atmosphere of the greenhouse, to the dry conditions of a living-room are often too much for the plants. Perhaps the best method in starting a collection is to buy tubers. These are normally available from January onwards, and if they are about two years old, they should have had one growing season and be up to two inches in diameter.

Early February is a good time to pot the tubers. Care should be taken to place them the right side up. The concave side is placed downwards, and the growing sprouts will come from the indented side. It is best to plant tubers at different times so that all do not mature during the same period. Those planted in early February should produce blooms from late May onwards so that by planting from February to April, a flowering period lasting until the late autumn can be assured.

Some growers allow more than one sprout to develop from each tuber, and this is usually satisfactory. If however, you intend to exhibit the plants when in flower, it is best to restrict the growths to one, selecting of course, the strongest, healthiest specimen. Unwanted shoots can easily be rubbed off or pinched out before they grow large. If, of course, one wishes to increase their stock it is worth letting some of the shoots grow to an inch or so high and then to carefully remove them and to pot them up as cuttings.

A special marker for spacing seedlings

For a potting mixture, use one made up of one part each of good soil, decayed manure, horticultural peat and silver sand with a little decayed manure or bone meal. Alternatively, the John Innes compost No. 2 can be used. One good sized tuber can be placed in a four or five-inch pot, although with extra large specimens, a bigger pot can be used. It is best however, not to use big pots to begin with, but to give the roots more room as they develop. A large pot of soil containing very few roots is liable to go sour, causing the roots to decay. Grown under healthy conditions, gloxinia tubers will last for a number of years, and three or four years is by no means unusual, although there have been instances when corms many years older continued to flower annually.

Always use clean pots. If they are new pots, soak them in water for some hours, otherwise the roots will quickly draw moisture from the soil to the detriment of the plant. Good drainage is required and apart from a few pieces of broken crocks at the bottom, a few small lumps of charcoal placed over the crocks before the compost is put in, will be of help.

Then fill the pot about three parts full of compost making it fairly firm. Set the tubers in the centre of the pot adding more soil until the tuber is covered. Do not bury the tuber deeply otherwise moisture may settle in the indented centre, and wet soil will lead to decay. While it is important for the compost not to be wet, it should be nicely moist at potting time, and if this is so, it will be sufficient to give the pots a sprinkling of water from a rosed can after planting is finished. This will make sure the tubers are closely surrounded by soil.

If more moisture is required before there is top growth, it is best to stand the pots in a pan of water having the chill off, and to let them stay there, until the top of the soil is just moist. The planted pots can then be placed in the cooler part of the greenhouse or in a south facing window, where after a while, the top growths will push through the surface.

Growth is fairly quick during the spring and summer, but naturally not so fast during colder periods. From a spring planting, it will usually be possible to see quite nice growths after three or four weeks. According to temperatures flower buds will appear within ten to twelve weeks onwards, and very often the plants are in full bloom within eighteen weeks or so from the time of planting.

Do not subject the plants to direct sunlight. When they have to stand on the greenhouse staging they should be given some shading during the sunniest weather.

The aim should be to produce short, stocky, free flowering plants, and not tall, spindly specimens. The latter are most likely to develop if the plants are kept in dull light, for although gloxinias should not be kept in full sun, they do like plenty of good light at all times.

Another point to observe in securing good shaped plants, is to turn them round from time to time, so that development is even. If left in one position they will gradually grow towards the light resulting in a poor shaped plant. Kept under good conditions the individual flowers will last up to a fortnight and when good plants are seen with several flowers opened at the same time, they are most impressive.

It should be remembered that gloxinias are natives of the jungle where there is a humid atmosphere coupled with heat. Therefore the aim should be to provide somewhat similar conditions. They do not object to slightly lower temperatures at night, in fact this seems to be helpful. Experience shows that where plants are grown indoors, in centrally heated rooms, they do not do quite so well as where other types of heating are used. These allow the temperature to fall at night-time. Gloxinias like light and fresh air, but not draughts.

From the time the young plants begin to develop, they will need watching for watering. Really good tubers do, of course, contain moisture which lasts them a considerable time, but they must never want for water, otherwise the tubers will shrivel and the plants will suffer.

While watering can be done from the top or the bottom of the pot the latter is the best method, where only a few plants are concerned. Pots are set in shallow vessels of water, so that moisture seeps through until the top soil feels moist to the touch. Do not water every day. It is best to give occasional waterings when necessary but not daily sprinklings as are sometimes practised. During the dull days of winter, plants need less water, but in warm weather, they will need a considerable amount, since apart from the root requirements, moisture is lost from the leaves through evaporation.

If you have to leave your plants for some days, they should be well watered first, and may then be stood in larger pots with damp moss or similar material placed between the two pots, as well as on the top soil. In this condition, and out of the sun, they will remain unharmed for two or three weeks. Alternatively, the pots can be stood on blocks of wood which in turn are placed in shallow vessels of water. The moisture will then seep up to the drainage hole from where the roots can make use of it.

D*

CHAPTER SEVENTEEN

Caring for the Plants

SINCE THE increased number of flowers depends upon the corm developing larger year by year, any little extra attention that is given will be well repaid. Gloxinias, do not multiply by producing off-sets, as do many subjects. They normally grow larger and become more free flowering as they grow older.

Gloxinias can be planted out of doors in favourable positions during the summer and where this is so they usually grow into really good sturdy plants. They can be kept in their pots and plunged in the ground where they have shade from direct sun. They usually make quite quick growth and this leads to really long stemmed flowers.

It is advisable to examine the plants frequently, to make sure that they do not lack moisture. If, when the flower buds are beginning to swell, the plants are taken into the living-room or cold greenhouse to open, they will provide a really wonderful display. They should be kept out of direct sunlight and should be placed where they have some humidity around them.

In sheltered, warm places, gloxinias can be used as temporary plants in window-boxes or in ornamental vases. Watch for aphis which sometimes settle in the centres of the plants and avoid bruising or breaking the leaves.

Water will not really harm gloxinia foliage, but it is advisable not to place the plants in the full sun when they are wet, or to stand the plants where water will drip on the foliage. at the same time as the sun is shining on it. Water and sun together, will scorch and scar the leaves, since the sun shining through the water, acts as a burning glass.

Gloxinias certainly do best when the foliage is clean. That is, not only clear of pests, but also free from dust and dirt. Since the leaves are hairy, dust readily adheres. It is, therefore best to spray the foliage with tepid water fairly frequently. The effect of this is to freshen the leaves, and generally improve the appearance of the plants.

Showing how to prepare a pot for Gloxinia tubers
Crocks first, then rough peat before soil

Sometimes the foliage decays at the base. This is usually the result of too much water and not enough warmth. Sometimes too, the tubers do not increase in size as they should, and this also is due to erratic watering, poor light, and lack of proper feeding materials. When the plants are starved, the foliage is sparse and since the tubers depend to a large extent on the leaves, for keeping them strong and healthy, and increasing their size, it is important to look after the foliage, even when the plants are out of flower.

The keeping of the plants in good light is also an advantage, as far as the colour of the blooms is concerned. Particularly in the case of rich coloured flowers, there is likely to be considerable variation in the colour shade if the plants are kept in dark corners, or other places where they are not amply supplied with light.

Saintpaulias are often grown under fluorescent lighting with great success and there is no reason at all why gloxinias should not be given similar treatment. In the United States they are sometimes grown with satisfaction in artificial light in homes where the natural light is not good.

Certainly practical experience is the best teacher, and it is worth-while beginning in a small way to discover whether one can execute successfully the simple technique involved. Suitable apparatus can be bought and after it has been set up it is really a matter of learning by experience how close to the lights the plants should be.

Experiments have shown that small plants need to be fairly close to the light if they are to receive the maximum benefit and a foot or so can be regarded as about right. In good conditions the leaves will develop well, increasing both in length and width. Once the flower buds begin to develop well, the plants should be moved away from the direct light toward the edge of the rays. There is little or no chance of the foliage being scorched, and although there is a fair amount of heat the soil in the containers does not dry out much more quickly than in the case of plants standing in the sunny greenhouse or living-room.

When watering, it is best to deal with the plants individually rather than using a water can and merely sprinkling the foliage. If finance allows, it is best to go for the longer lights rather than making up with several of the smaller ones. Whilst naturally some expense is involved in this method of growing, it need not be very costly, and should be well worth the amount expended, especially to the plant lover.

Among the more modern conveniences are automatic switches so that where the fluorescent light is not constantly needed, it is possible to arrange for the lights to be cut off at given times.

Not only is it possible to start with growing plants, but success has been achieved in raising plants from seed. Whereas sometimes with the normal method, seedlings take quite a long time to break through the surface, if the seed pans or boxes are kept under the fluorescent light, the seed will often germinate within ten days, making it possible to prick off the seedlings within a month from sowing.

CHAPTER EIGHTEEN

Species and Varieties

Species

The species are very difficult to obtain since most of the gloxinias in cultivation today are named hybrids.

Concinna, purple and white, growing two and a half to three feet high. Early.

Conspicua, heart-shaped hairy leaves, the cream trumpet is yellow inside and dotted purple.

Crassifolia. This, according to the Dictionary of Gardening issued by the Royal Horticultural Society, is a trade name given to one of the strains brought about by hybridisation nearly 100 years ago. The plants have ' round velvety thick leaves, plump short buds, large solid flowers, very wide at the mouth, but with a narrow tube. Colours range through the blues into shades of rose.

Diversiflora (variable) dwarf growing.

Glabra or fimbriata. White with yellow throat, spotted purple.

Guttata. Blue with speckled throat.

Helleri. White spotted red.

Maculata. The rather bell-shaped downy, purple-blue flowers are not unlike those of a Canterbury Bell.

Macrophylla. Very deep purple. The large flowers being well set off by the olive-green marked foliage, which is patterned with whitish veins, forming unusual plants of a slightly pyramidal shape.

Maximiliana. Very dainty creamy-white flowers, the inside is marked purple with yellow dots. Attractive glossy foliage.

Pallidiflora, attractive, pale blue flowers.

Passinghamii, synonymous with G. speciosa.

Regina. The handsome deep lavender flowers borne above the foliage, are of rather more dumpy appearance than the other species. The leaves circle the stem in opposite pairs and are beautifully veined silver-green.

Speciosa. The species most used to bring about many of todays named hybrids. Small neat, purple-blue flowers, long hairy pointed leaves with curled edges. Sometimes known as the Blue Slipper gloxinia.

Varieties

As the result of the great amount of work done in hybridising since the introduction of the gloxinia, there are now a great many varieties in cultivation, although they are not always readily available, unless one asks for them by name.

Some of the older types can still take their place with the newer introductions. They are given in alphabetical order although in some cases the habit of growth varies.

Blanche de Meru. Purplish-red with white throat.

Brunhilde. A large shining white flower with crinkled edges.

Crisper Meteor. A showy light scarlet with frilled petals.

Defiance. Rich clear red of pleasing appearance.

Emperor Frederick. Scarlet with broad pearly-white margin.

Emperor William. Rich pansy blue, with broad white margin.

Etoile de Feu. Shining cardinal-red.

Fire King. With striking flame-red flowers.

George Luxton. Of American origin. This produces flowers of which the inside is wine-red with lighter edges, the outside of these frilled flowers being clear pink.

Grandiflora. This is a strain taking in many separate colours and spotted hybrids.

Hollywood. A fine purple which seems to sparkle in the light.

Imperator. In shades of pink and rose, the foliage often assuming a reddish hue.

Mont Blanc. Clear white trumpet, rarely frilled.

Meteor. A reliable variety with light red flowers.

Prince Albert. Dark violet with white throat.

Queen Wilhelmina. Dainty pink with a showy velvet sheen.

Rhine. Light pink, of pleasing appearance.

Roi des Rouge. Striking shiny red flowers.

Star of Fire. See Etoile de Feu.

Switzerland. Scarlet-cerise, with white ruffled edges.

Tannenberg. Clear brilliant red.

Tigrina Perfecta. Spotted and laced flowers on a red ground.

Trudy. A named Buell hybrid of which the main colour is white, the variegated red markings adding to its beauty.

Violacea. Deep velvety bluish-purple.

Waterloo. A well known variety, the showy scarlet flowers being ruffled at the edges.

There are various hybrids of Belgian origin which are not always easy to obtain in Britain. The Buell hybrids, named for their originator Albert Buell, produce extra large flowers, many of which have additional petals which are ruffled making them especially attractive. The colour range is wide taking in many unusual pinks, honey tones and orchid shades.

There are a number of gloxinias which have proved particularly useful for exhibition purposes. These include: Bacchus, deep wine colour; Blue Cloud, white, edged pale blue; Duchess, purple, edged white; Duke of York, scarlet, edged white; Grenadier, deep glowing scarlet; Her Majesty, pure white; Pink Princess, white edged pink; Royal Purple, rich velvety colour; and the Spotted and Netted hybrids, in dainty fascinating shades.

Gloxinera, this is a name given to a bigeneric hybrid between a gloxinia and Gesnera pyramidalis. The latter is the pollen parent.

This plant was grown more than seventy years ago, by the

once famous firm of Messrs. Veitch of Chelsea. It was
described as having foliage similar to a gloxinia, the leaves
being rather succulent, and covered with fine hairs. The
flowers were of good size, and of a bright scarlet tinged with
magenta. This plant does not appear to be available today,
and would be difficult to find even in botanic garden
collections of plants.

CHAPTER NINETEEN

Propagating Gloxinias

THERE ARE various ways of propagating gloxinias, and the easiest is to sow seeds. This can be done at various times of the year, although if the seed is sown in January or February, the resultant plants should flower from the late summer onwards. If sowing is delayed until July, the first blooms are unlikely to appear much before the following March or April.

Use a good fine seed sowing mixture containing loam, leaf mould or peat, and silver sand, all of which should be passed through a fine sieve. Alternatively, the John Innes seed compost is suitable. The seed is very fine and therefore needs sowing with great care. To help in even distribution, it is a good plan to mix the seed with a little fine silver sand. Use seed pans, pots or trays – nothing deep being required, first providing some drainage material before putting in the soil mixture.

Some growers sterilise the compost in an endeavour to prevent any possibility of the seedlings damping off. If the plants are grown under clean healthy conditions, and they are pricked out early, being watered with care, there should be little trouble from damping off. This is a fungus disease normally classed as botrytis. It flourishes in a close, humid atmosphere.

As far as possible provide a temperature of 60 to 70 degrees F. avoiding a dry atmosphere. Although this is the ideal, it is possible to raise gloxinias from seed with very little warmth. There are recorded incidents of seedlings being raised when the boxes have been stood on the radio. This seems to give an appreciated bottom heat, leading

113

to quick germination. Water with the utmost care both to prevent the surface soil caking and the seedlings from damping off.

One way of lessening the necessity of watering, is to sow the seeds in a pot in the usual way, and then to stand it into a larger pot packing the inside space between the two pots with moist sphagnum moss. Cover the sown receptacles with glass and paper until germination occurs, for if the surface soil dries out the seedlings are liable to shrivel.

When buying in seed it may appear that there is only a small quantity of seed in the packet, but since the seed is so tiny a small quantity really consists of a very large number.

As soon as the seedlings have four leaves. they should be pricked off into other pots or boxes using a mixture of loam, silver sand and a good proportion of peat or leaf mould, with some finely sifted manure or bone meal. From this time, growth is normally fairly rapid and small tubers will develop. This means that the plants will soon need potting individually.

When pricking out, it will be helpful to use a pair of tweezers to save bruising the foliage and for the first and certainly for subsequent moves, always hold the seedlings by the leaves. This prevents bruising and normally ensures that the leaves are not broken. This is even less likely if each little plant is loosened before being lifted.

Freshly planted seedlings should be kept out of direct sunlight, otherwise they will soon begin to look sickly and may die. No fertiliser should be applied until the flower buds begin to swell, then give a liquid organic feed, applying this at ten day intervals, until the flowers open.

Although many of them are so fragile, seedlings can usually put up with many adverse conditions. Very often they start with the disadvantage of insufficient light when they first appear through the surface of the soil. This results in weakness which renders them more susceptible to disease and other adverse conditions.

No seedling likes to be subjected to a rapid change of

temperature, and particularly in the case of those raised in a propagator, the change from the close humid conditions there to the exposure of open greenhouse should be spread over a few days. It could of course, be started by opening the propagator a little and gradually reducing the shading until the seedlings become accustomed to full light. The standing of the trays or pans of seedlings on a shelf near the glass will prevent them from becoming drawn. They must not be allowed to dry out.

Pricking off should not be delayed, for overcrowding leads to thin stems, poor foliage and a tendency to damping off. Early pricking off gives the seedlings the chance to recover quickly and make a good root system without which strong top growth will not develop.

Sometimes it is necessary to remove some seedlings before the others are ready for transplanting. There is always the possibility of root damage, but this is not likely to be severe if the plants are moved whilst they are small for them, there will be no tangling of the fibres.

Damping off causes the stalks of the plants to rot and shrivel at ground level. The seedlings then topple over and die. The use of Cheshunt Compound in water when this is necessary, will greatly reduce the possibility of damping off, although it will not cure affected plants. Care is needed however, in the application of Cheshunt Compound, since too many applications may cause the little leaves to become somewhat discoloured and it has also been found that growth has slowed up and the plants then become stunted.

Always prick out the seedlings in the warm and do not leave the roots exposed. for if this happens even for a short period, the seedlings will suffer, and may easily die. It is best to water the trays and pots a day before pricking out is done.

The water used must always be clean and it is a good plan whenever possible to have a tank inside the greenhouse. This can be used to store the rain-water collected from the roof. This water is so much better for plants than tap water. It is important to keep the inside tank clean, and it is always advisable to cover the top, both to prevent soil and rubbish from falling in, and to stop algae forming. This green growth is not likely to appear if the tank is kept shaded.

Not the least advantage in having a tank in the house is that the water used is more or less of the same temperature as the soil being watered. This lessens any possibility of a check which can occur when very cold water is used.

To increase stock more rapidly than from seed, it is sometimes possible to split the tubers and plant each section separately. Gloxinias form a number of eyes, and each section must have at least one eye, and a good portion of tuber if it is to produce a really good specimen. It is therefore important to ensure before cutting, that there really is a sprout in each section. After dividing the tubers, dust the cut portion with sulphur powder, and plant as soon as possible.

Another simple way of obtaining a stock or of increasing a particularly good variety, is through leaf cuttings. For this purpose, fairly young leaves in good, healthy condition should be selected. Carefully take off the stem, if possible with a little heal of old skin at the bottom. Then plant the leaves in a pan or tray of really sandy compost, or it is possible to root the leaves in water. Usually leaf cuttings soon form a new tuber at the base, although in the case of plants rooted in water, the leaf itself may wither or even die, but by that time the base of the leaf will have broadened and a tuber will soon form. In this case, do not disturb the compost, for the new growth will be seen pushing through the soil after some weeks.

Some gardeners put each leaf cutting in a separate pot and cover this with a bell glass or even a polythene bag, since these maintain a moist atmosphere, which encourages early and good rooting.

Another method of propagating leaves is to plant them in the usual way in pots of sandy compost and stand these in larger pots with a layer of moist sand or sphagnum moss between the two pots. This ensures that the compost does not dry out and an even supply of moisture is always a great assistance in rooting leaf cuttings.

Occasionally, gloxinias are propagated by laying selected leaves face downwards on the surface of boxes or pans of moist compost. The thicker veins are severed and the leaves can be kept in position by placing small stones on them. If this can be done in a propagating case, the warm, humid atmosphere will be of great assistance in early root formation. As soon as the tubers can be seen swelling nicely, each plant can be moved to a separate pot. Really good leaves will normally supply five or six strong healthy young plants.

When the little tubers are of pea size and this can easily be seen, since they form near the surface soil, separate each rooted portion. Do this with a sharp knife leaving a little piece of leaf with each part. If leaf vein severing is done in early spring and the growth is good, it is possible that some flowers may be produced the first year before the young plants become dormant. When the foliage begins to discolour, gradually withhold water but do not knock the plants out of the pots as is usual with older specimens.

Although experiments in propagation have been made with colchicine, this is not really a job for the amateur gardener. Certainly colchicine slows down the rooting progress and plants raised by this method often make freakish growth. There is, of course, always the possibility that an odd looking plant with some good characteristics may be produced and then it is necessary to discover by propagating such specimens, whether the characteristics are fixed and are likely to be repeated in successive generations.

It is not always necessary to re-pot gloxinias annually particularly when a good, fairly rich compost, is used initially. Where re-potting is not done, it is a good plan to carefully remove the top inch or two of compost and replace it with fresh enriched material. Gloxinias prefer rather acid soil and it is therefore best to avoid using a compost in which lime is present.

CHAPTER TWENTY

Exhibiting the Plants

IN MOST horticultural shows, there is a class for pot plants. This class is not generally supported as much as it might be. The gloxinia is a first-class subject for exhibiting, and well grown specimens always create attention, especially those with clear, bold colours, some of which are attractively netted. So often one sees plants on the show bench, which with a little attention, could have been greatly improved. It is not always possible to present perfect specimens, but so much can be done to make the plants catch the favourable eye of the judge.

The Horticultural Show Handbook issued by the Royal Horticultural Society, gives guidance as to what are considered meritorious points, and also faults which are to be eradicated where possible. The following is an extract from the handbook, and is quoted by permission of the Secretary of the Royal Horticultural Society.

Meritorious. A vigorous and floriferous plant, with erect flowers. Flowers having a circular outline; with rounded overlapping lobes, and throats in proportion to the length of the lobes. Clear colours and distinct markings. Healthy foliage, of good substance, undamaged and clean.

Defective. A weakly plant, with few flowers; or with flowers which are not erect. Flowers with an irregular outline, or having lobes which do not overlap, or having disproportionately wide throats. Undecided colours, and indistinct markings. Thin, pale, damaged or spotted leaves. For the plant, 6 points. Form of flower, 5 points. Colour, 5 points. Foliage, 4 points. Total 20 points. The fact that plants with all the good points mentioned cannot be shown, should not discourage the grower from exhibiting the plants he has available thus giving pleasure to show visitors.

Most gloxinias will throw up a number of shoots and the plants intended for exhibition should have these shoots reduced to the strongest one, when they are about a couple of inches high. Once the plants have recovered from this thinning out and the leaves begin to flatten out in the way which is typical of gloxinias, the plants should be moved to the larger pots in which they are to be exhibited.

The size of the pot largely depends upon the plant. Sometimes a good sized specimen can be shown in a five-inch pot. In other cases a six-inch or even a seven-inch pot will be needed. The foliage is quite substantial and a small pot might easily detract from the appearance of the plant when placed on the exhibition table. The leaves grow quickly and on a really good plant, will completely cover the top of the pot. With the many flowers usually produced, this will create an imposing effect. Ideally, the plants should be kept where there is a night temperature around 65 degrees F.

The exhibitor may sometimes have to use plants which are not quite in tip top condition. The aim should be however, to have available on show day, specimens on which the blooms are fresh and the petals firm and rather stiff looking. For preference, there should also be a number of flower buds at various stages of expansion. Take care not to break the foliage which is rather brittle, particularly in the case of some varieties.

As with many types of plants the first blooms are often a little inferior and on exhibition plants they should be removed. As a guide, between six or seven weeks are needed from the time the flower bud is just visible until it is in the finest condition. This time is liable to vary, being largely dependent on temperature and general culture. It will however, give guidance regarding timing, particularly when some of the earlier buds and flowers have to be removed.

If the show is at a distant place the transport question is something which needs careful consideration. The flowers on any gloxinia plant which rub against their neighbours, will soon become bruised by friction. For this reason it is advisable, in fact necessary, to keep the flowers and stems from moving or being shaken in any way, by placing cotton-wool or some white tissue paper between the flowers. Do this in such a way that the inner sides of the bells touch it.

Then insert two small but sturdy sticks, on opposite sides of the pot, so that the top of the supports is just above the level of the flower height. After this, place thickish bands of tissue paper around the outside of the flowers so as to form a bunch without, of course, nipping or bruising the blooms.

The bunches should be fastened to the two supports and will thereby be held firmly in position. This will prevent the flowers from moving or becoming damaged in any way. Each pot needs packing separately in a good strong container, with sufficient soft packing material between each pot to take the jar or rub which inevitably occurs when the plants are conveyed by road or rail.

If the plants are being taken on a journey by the grower himself, he will be able to take the necessary care in not letting the vehicle stand in hot sunshine. If this does happen, even for a short time, it can have an adverse effect on the plants causing them to lose their natural liveliness. This is one reason why commercial growers who are sending plants such as gloxinias and saintpaulias on a journey, prefer to travel by night when it is cooler, and when it is usually possible to make the journey in a shorter time.

As soon as convenient, the plants should be carefully unpacked and lightly shaken so that the leaves and flowers fall into their natural positions again. Once again, the utmost care is needed in handling the pots so that there is no likelihood of bruising or other damage. Place the gloxinias in full light but out of direct sunshine.

When setting up the plants allow plenty of time, for so often even when tip-top plants are available, poor staging due to rushing the job, loses points and causes disappointments which need not occur.

While it is not usual for gloxinias to be staged in a show

as cut flowers, it can be done. When it is, the blooms always attract attention. They do, of course, need to be carefully placed in a suitable bowl and because they are light and airy, it is best to fasten each stem by pressing the base on to a sharp spike. Pin holders as used in floral decoration bowls are suitable for this purpose.

In this way, each individual flower can be easily looked into and the attractive and delicate throat markings can be fully appreciated. It is probably true that few people have ever really looked into a gloxinia bloom and have therefore missed seeing some most beautiful tracery which is to be found on the inside of the flowers.

Some foliage should be included and unless the show schedule indicates otherwise, there is no reason why some other type of suitable greenery should not be included. However, this should not protrude in any way. The exhibit is of gloxinia flowers and it is these with their own foliage, which should be in evidence.

If it *is* decided to cut the flowers for the exhibition, the job needs doing with care. The stems must be placed in water immediately, otherwise they will become limp and flabby. Even although they may subsequently draw up water, they do not assume their original shape and good appearance. Then, of course, they must be handled with great care so that the velvety surfaces are not bruised or broken in any way.

Obviously, any and all flowers to be cut should be in first class condition and just coming up to their best. To cut a flower which has passed its zenith means that by the time the judges see it, it will not look as it should.

Make sure that the inside of the trumpets do not become soiled. Since the centre of the flowers where the stamens are, is usually sticky, dust easily adheres. It is therefore advisable to cover the flowers with tissue paper or something similar while they are being conveyed to the show place.

CHAPTER TWENTY-ONE

Pests, Diseases and Disorders

WHILST THE gloxinia is not particularly susceptible to pests, diseases or disorders, there are sometimes problems which arise in regard to culture. It is wise to be aware of the possible troubles which might affect these plants.

Aphids, will attack almost any plant, and although they seldom settle on gloxinias, they occasionally do so. The green type, usually referred to as green fly, may alight on the centre of the plant and here, as well as on the undersides of the leaves, they suck the sap from the plant, causing the foliage to cockle or curl, become pale, and fall prematurely. Sometimes the leaves take on a spotted appearance. It is advisable to look over the plants at frequent intervals, so that these pests do not gain a hold. They can normally be cleared with liquid derris or pyrethum.

Tarsonemid or cyclamen mite varies in colour from a whitish shade to a light brown. These pests too, live on the lower sides of the leaves, from which they suck the juice, causing curling and brittleness, the foliage turning a purplish colour. The plants become distorted and the flower buds wither. It is really best to cut off affected parts and to dust the remaining growth with D.D.T. As a rule the plants then form new leaves which so long as the mite is not present on other plants nearby will develop into really healthy growth. These mites which are not unlike red spiders can also be cleared with a weak solution of summer petroleum emulsion.

Thrips are perhaps the most persistent pest likely to attack and they can do a tremendous amount of damage if allowed to gain a hold. They are small active insects, and vary from yellow to black in colour. These pests too, suck the sap from the leaves, stems and flowers, causing them to become deformed and to develop a silvery or brownish sheen. Sometimes the flower buds discolour and fail to open. Affected plants can be sprayed with a nicotine wash, badly spoiled leaves are best removed and burned, while in the glasshouse, a D.D.T. aerosol is effective. Attacks are most likely to occur when conditions are hot and dry.

Sometimes flowers become deformed. This is normally caused when temperatures vary greatly in the spring. Such oddities are only a temporary occurrence and usually, the plants return to their normal development after a week or two.

Another trouble is known as wilt. In this case, the leaves look lifeless and drooping and it might be thought that the plants need water. On examination however, it is usually found that the compost is moist enough. The trouble is a disease which attacks the plants just above soil level and this type of fungus or botrytis infection can cause the whole stem to collapse.

Therefore, the reason that the leaves become wilted is that the sap has ceased to flow up the stem. The best plan is to remove affected foliage, carefully cutting off the piece of tuber from where the stem springs and dusting the wound with yellow sulphur powder. If wilt occurs before the plants are very large, the tuber can be moved into a new pot complete with fresh compost.

Then there is the condition sometimes know as bud blast. This is seen in the shoots shrivelling, becoming discoloured and lifeless. This condition has several causes and includes waterlogged roots, the use of very cold water, a close, dry atmosphere and an over-rich soil. The trouble can sometimes be seen as a discolouration behind the calyx, and it is best to remove all flower stems affected by bud blast. Good general cultivation is the answer to this trouble and if the air does not become too dry and the compost is kept moist without becoming waterlogged, there should be no fear of this disorder.

There are occasions when a tuber has been planted properly and yet fails to produce shoots. Sometimes such tubers will remain quite firm for many weeks. It may simply be that they are slow starters and after a further period will start into life. If of course, such tubers become soft and spongy they will be useless. This tuber rot is of fungus origin and it is unlikely that even if the soft portions are cut out, the tuber will prove really satisfactory.

In the early stages perhaps, where small pieces can be removed and the wounds are dusted with yellow sulphur, the disease may be overcome. This condition is brought about by overwatering, low temperatures and planting the tuber too deeply or pressing it too firmly in the compost. The latter of course, prevents soil aeration so necessary for root formation.

CHAPTER TWENTY-TWO

The Origin of the African Violet

ALTHOUGH THE saintpaulia is undoubtedly an old plant, its modern history begins with its discovery towards the end of the last century by the District Governor of Usambara in East Africa. His name was Adalbert Emil Walter Redliffe le Tanneux von St. Paul-Illaire.

Seeds, and possibly plants were sent to the Governor's father Baron Walter St. Paul-Illaire. This man, realising the importance of his son's discovery brought it to the notice of the Director of the Royal Botanic Gardens at Herrenhausen, who was Herman Wendland, who issued the description of the species and named it Saintpaulia ionantha. It seems likely that plants were also sent to Botanical Gardens in this country, including those at Kew and Cambridge.

The genus name of course commemorated the name of the discoverer and the species name indicating that the flowers are like the violet.

There are several places in Tanganyika where these plants grow, the altitude varying from under fifty to more than 3,000 feet. Here we are told, the plants root in the crevices of rocks, where humus matter has gathered or been formed by decaying matter falling into such places. A certain amount of shade is present in these places thus giving a clue to the conditions the plants like. That is, plenty of light but not direct sunshine.

It was not until almost forty years ago that saintpaulias became the interest of commercial growers. First of all there was an American firm in Los Angeles where a very large number of plants were raised, but only a few retained as being worth-while. From this small number there was developed very large quantities of plants which have been distributed far and wide. Subsequently other firms became interested in this lovely subject.

The African Violet is of course now grown on a very large scale in the United States. In fact, it was the African Violet Society of America founded about twenty years ago, which brought saintpaulias into such great popularity. This Society now consists of many thousands of members who share their knowledge, information and individual data, which gives help and guidance to growers of all standards. Much information is spread through the quarterly Journal published by the Society.

There is also an African Violet Society in this country, which is most active and increasing its influence annually. Much help is given through the regular meetings and lectures held, also through the literature distributed. Anyone who is keen on growing these plants should certainly join the Society, and thus gain full and the latest information regarding the growing of African Violets in all their stages.

There are a number of misconceptions about these plants. Firstly, they are not related to the ordinary violets. Saintpaulias belong to the gesneriaceae family, which includes such better known subjects as gloxinias, streptocarpus, ramonda and others. It is therefore useless to think of crossing a saintpaulia with a violet.

Then it is often said that this is a temperamental plant for the amateur to grow. The fact is, it is no more difficult than very many other plants. In addition, it can be grown in the living-room continually and does not need to be taken into the greenhouse after short periods in the house. It is certainly an easy subject to propagate. It is long flowering and this makes it especially valuable.

The African Violet is definitely here to stay as a good pot plant and general houseplant subject. It has many first-class qualities, being attractive both in foliage and flower. When its requirements are understood it is easy to grow and yet, because it can be a little temperamental, its culture provides much interest to the keen, though not necessarily skilled grower.

African Violets are not slow to show their dislike of strong sunshine, improper watering, draughts and dirty foliage. It is therefore necessary to frequently look over the plants to ensure that they do not suffer from any of these things and in fact, the success or failure in cultivating these plants is in the grower's hands.

It is a good plan to purchase an initial stock of plants in the spring or summer when living-room or greenhouse conditions are likely to be most favourable for good cultivation. This plant is one which can have too much sunshine, although not too much light. It is therefore helpful if the plants are kept where they are out of midday sun, but where they do get full light. If they catch the sunlight in the early morning or evening it will certainly not harm the plants. A north or north-east or even east window is an excellent site for this plant, which can be had in bloom from May to September, sometimes longer. The plant will soon indicate whether the position given is suitable. A point to remember is that whilst during the winter months the window position chosen is ideal, in the summer, it may become extremely hot and dry which the plants cannot stand. Then it will be necessary to provide some shading and this can be done, in several ways, including the putting up of fine net curtains or something similar.

The amount of water the plants need depends on the temperature as well as the type of compost used. Then of course, there is the size and vigour of the plant in relation to the size of the pot used.

It is helpful if lukewarm water is used. Never give water to a plant which already has moist soil conditions. If plants are kept on gravel trays, they should not be allowed to stand so that water touches the bottom of the pot.

Since these plants flower so freely, they are liable to become exhausted if not fed well. Therefore, a fortnightly feed of an organic liquid fertiliser should be applied and both Maxicrop and Liquinure have proved valuable. Never apply it stronger than recommended by the manufacturers and as far as possible, keep the liquid off the foliage.

The question is often asked how soon and how long will saintpaulias flower. It is impossible to give precise times since so much depends on growing conditions. It is worth noting that saintpaulias can be seen exhibited at the Royal Horticultural Society's shows throughout the greater part of the year, which is certainly an indication of what this plant can do. First requisites for continuous flowering include plenty of light and also direct sunshine in the winter, with a temperature which does not fall below 60 degrees F.

When the plants are kept in the living-room where air conditions are fairly dry during the winter, attention must be given to providing humidity. This can be done by standing the pots on damp peat or sand while they can be lightly sprayed with tepid water once or twice a week. Whatever spraying is done it should be carried out early in the day, so that moisture is off the leaves by the late afternoon.

To keep the plants flowering continuously, feed regularly with weak liquid manure and it is of further help to keep the plants slightly pot bound, since this has the effect of restricting excessive leaf growth and diverting the strength of the plant to flower production. Plants must not of course, be left in the same pots once they have obviously become too large for the receptacles. Otherwise, they will starve, the flowers become poor, the foliage pale and the fibrous roots will decay. It is a mistake to move the plants from small to large pots in one effort. They should be re-potted to one size larger at a time. Soil in large pots where there are few roots will soon go sour, with harmful results to the plants.

Saintpaulias ionantha has been valued as a pot plant for many years and no one who has grown it with reasonable success would like to be without it. Its bright and cheerful blue flowers when they appear during the long and often dreary winter days, provide colour when it is most lacking.

It is not surprising therefore, that this plant is now being grown more widely than ever before and that by the con-

27. *Left*: Standard Rose-form Flower.

28. A Group of Double Begonias.

29. *Above*: Begonia Multiflora,
    Golden Showers.

30. *Right*: Double Crested Begonia,

31. Double Begonias flowering in the open in September, only 8 months after sowing seed!
Photo by courtesy Blackmore & Langdon Ltd.

32. Begonias in out-door beds in flower in September.
Photo by courtesy Blackmore & Langdon Ltd.

33. Specimen Ruffled Begonia.

34. Ruffled Camellia-Flowered Begonia.

stant introduction of new varieties and the energetic activities of the Saintpaulia and Houseplant Society the value of this plant is becoming known to a very large number of people who are finding it a rewarding subject to grow in the living-room as well as the greenhouse.

Flower pot with glass or plastic cover

As the chairman of the Society wrote in a recent bulletin: 'every now and again the question arises, which varieties of saintpaulia do you recommend for the beginner? Alternatively, one is asked to name six or more varieties. These questions call for a straightforward answer, that is to name varieties which are commonly reported to be good doers. It would be possible to give a variety of answers to these questions, answers which, though not so straightforward, containing at least an element of the truth. If you have the right conditions almost all varieties are easy, but if your conditions are not right, then all are difficult – except as short lived plants.'

E

CHAPTER TWENTY-THREE

General Cultivation

FOR THE production of best quality flowers, African Violets depend on the light, temperature and humidity they receive. In their native habitat, they are used to long periods of daylight and although the plants are subjected to tropical sun, they normally grow on rocky crevices and in the shade of tropical forests.

This means that they do not require a very high degree of light intensity. They do not like direct summer sun. If therefore a south facing window is the only position available, some light protection should be given during hours of bright sunshine. During spells of dull weather from autumn to spring, they should be exposed to any sun that is available.

It is easy to think of the tropics as being very hot but where these plants grow on the mountain ranges of Tanganyika, the temperature is lower, and at night it drops considerably. The prevailing winds are usually heavily laden with moisture. This tells us that the plants are likely to succeed best where there is a humid atmosphere.

In the greenhouse or living-room, there are at least two good ways of providing humidity. The potted plants can be placed on a bed of shingles or similar material, in a container of some kind, which is kept moist, although the level of the water should be kept below the bottom of the pot.

Alternatively, the pots of saintpaulias can be placed in larger pots, including the ornamental glazed type. The space between the two pots should be filled with moist peat or sphagnum moss, which must never be allowed to become dry. A temperature of around 65 degrees F. and 10 degrees lower at night, will be satisfactory, although it is advisable to move the plants from window sills or other places where they are near the glass, during the winter. So often, window sill plants are left in position when the curtains are drawn. The space behind the blinds where the plants are, then becomes the coldest part of the room.

Regarding the size of the final pots, all growers wish to have plants as large as possible but it is a mistake to keep plants growing in big pots when there are only few roots. Under such circumstances, the soil is liable to become sour, leading to the decay of the roots and sickness of the plants. On the other hand, the plants should never become pot bound for this results in starvation followed by weak growth.

The best plan is to pot on the plants as soon as the roots fill the pot. This means several moves as growth progresses. Flowering plants in three and a half-inch pots look superb but if they are very strong growing, they may need four and a half or five-inch pots.

Many growers use pans as opposed to pots. The former are not so deep and should be suitable for African Violets, since, as we have said, they grow naturally on rocky crevices where there is little depth of soil. They are obviously shallow rooting and do not require any great depth of soil. When pots are used by commercial growers the lower portion of the pot is usually filled with peat, sphagnum moss or brick chippings, thus reducing the depth of soil as well as providing adequate drainage.

The watering of plants is a subject which always occupies the attention of the pot plant grower. No simple programme will adequately meet all needs, for different plants require different amounts of moisture. The same plant has different water requirements according to the time of year and where it is grown. Humidity, temperature, the atmosphere and the compost used are all considerations which have to be taken into account.

Certainly the watering of a pot plant is one of the most important factors in its well being. Many plants are killed by incorrect watering, probably more so than by wrong temperatures or incorrect compost. The majority of the food the plant needs comes from the soil. It is the function of the roots to extract what the plant needs and this can only be done when the substances are in solution.

The solution taken in by the roots passes through the cells into the plant, through the root system of the stems, and then into the leaves. The foliage is really a delicate factory which changes the simple substances supplied by the roots into complex chemicals which are passed to all parts of the plant to assist in further growing. Therefore, if water is not available at the roots, the plants will die.

In addition, leaves have tiny pores which allow water to be given off in the form of vapour. This means that there is almost constant movement of water through the plant from the soil and subsequently into the atmosphere. The actual intake of water by the roots is controlled by the presence of air in the soil as well as moisture.

Obviously a waterlogged compost is one in which all the area is occupied by water with no room for air. Without air, the roots rot and the plant dies. This is why too much water is quite as harmful as too little, a point often overlooked by some pot plant growers who keep the pots almost water-logged. Soil temperature is also important having a great effect on development. A warm soil will need more water than a cold one.

There are various methods of applying water and its application both in the top of the pot in the usual way or by standing the pot in vessels of shallow water which seeps up from the drainage hole, are if properly carried out, quite satisfactory.

Recently attention has been given to the capillary watering of pot plants. This can readily be done through a bed of sand kept moist by an automatic feed system.

Wick feeding has, of course, been practised for a long time but there certainly seems to be a future in the capillary method. One of the most used at present is the Keyluter system based on that developed by Mr. Chilcott of Brent. In this system, water from the mains, supplies a tank mounted several feet above the bench and this tank supplies water at lowest pressure to a float valve at bench level and controls the water level in the feeder cups.

In the Humex system, sand is contained in fibreglass trays instead of being spread on an asbestos sheet on the bench. The mains fed tank is at bench level and has an adjustable ball-cock to control the water level. The feed to the sand is from a continuous trough along the front of the tray. Trays can be connected end to end with short pieces of tube. The Humex tank is supplied with a rack which can be screwed to a support and a piece of flexible tubing connects it to the tray.

Growth of green algae and also black mould on the surface of the sand is likely with any wet sand system. Since it is not easy to control this trouble by chemical means, it is worth covering the sand immediately around the pots with black polythene. The remaining sand can be covered with a thin layer of spongy matting to allow some evaporation. The value of this material is that it can be washed from time to time. One must be careful to avoid overlapping the edge of the bench in order to prevent drips.

Obviously if watering is important so is the compost and as a start, some crocking at the base of the pot is advisable. Before use, the pot should be clean and well washed. Clay pots which are still probably the best containers, are of course, porous and in time, unless they are washed the pores of the pot will become clogged and can only be cleaned by washing.

The compost for both saintpaulias and gloxinias should contain sand and peat (or leaf mould) to encourage good drainage. For preference the sand should be coarse river washed sand. Never use builders sand, for this has binding properties and these will impede and not help drainage. The addition of a little charcoal will be a great help in keeping the compost sweet.

Plants do, of course, require more moisture in the summer months than in the spring or autumn, and much less in the winter. In the summer, provided the right compost is used it will be found helpful to syringe between the plant pots on the staging since this increases the atmospheric humidity.

The rate of transpiration is controlled by humidity in the atmosphere as well as the temperature. Then, of course, ventilation and the amount of water available to the plants also influence transpiration.

Growing under Artificial Light

African Violets can be grown under artificial light and Mr. G. W. Wicks, the African Violet specialist of Mapperley Nurseries, Nottingham has given me permission to quote on this subject from the splendid brochure his firm issue.

' The type of irradiation may differ in that incandescent light may be used or fluorescent will be equally effective (and considerably cheaper to run). While in the U.S.A. I saw many such installations, the largest in Minnesota with over 200 four-foot fluorescent fixtures each with two forty watt daylight tubes. The grower had four lots of plants growing on stages one above the other.

Whereas some five or six years ago this method was in its infancy and experimental stage, now the whole aspect has changed and from our own series of tests we can assure you that it is possible to bloom an African Violet for a full twelve months without cessation from the time it first comes into flower. Our experiments have totalled some thousands of plants and have exceeded all expectations.

Daylight fluorescent tubes are used – five-foot are eighty watts; four-foot are forty watts, and on our latest small tray two-foot are twenty watts only. All are suspended some fifteen inches above the top of the pots and the fitment containing the tubes has a curved enamelled reflector. In the large installation (nine lamps of four and five feet) which is installed in a north room with a medium sized window (incidentally for all practical purposes this window is useless for providing light for the African Violets) a time clock switches the lights on for fifteen hours a day and thermo tubes controlled with a thermostat set at 60 degrees F. keep a reasonable temperature. The installation is erected in ' dexion ' with galvanised trays some two inches deep with approximately one inch of quarter inch gravel lining the bottom of the trays, and warm water is used to keep the water level just below the gravel surface. This is of prime importance for this water level gives that humidity so essential to healthy African Violets. It also tends to reduce the amount of direct watering the plants need.

Feeding with ' Liquinure ' or ' Maxicrop ' is practised, and given at shorter intervals in the spring and summer months (once every other time) with possibly half the quantity in autumn and winter, although it all depends on the plant's need.

The two-foot installation mentioned is one that we adapted for use in a dining-room which is equipped with one of the all-night burning fires. Through all the inclement weather the plants bloomed profusely and flourished beyond expectation. It was no longer an experiment, but an accomplished fact, a real indoor garden which is still in regular use.

The placing of the lamps is important, for wrongly sited, they will cause plants to grow upward instead of outward in the normally attractive rosette form so characteristic of saintpaulias.

Varieties with very dark green foliage should be placed so that they are up to fifteen inches below fluorescent lamps. Those with lighter green and variegated foliage, should also be at least the same distance and in addition, should not be placed directly under the lamps but kept in such a position that the light does not shine straight on them.

Too much light may cause the plant to produce an extra bunchy, central growth of poor colour and it may also encourage the variegated leaved sorts to produce plain green foliage. As experiments continue to be made it will no doubt be possible to perfect this method of culture but meanwhile, regular examination of the plants should be made so that those under fluorescent lighting do not become loose growing, sprawling or produce bunched growth.

Whether you use one section of fluorescent lighting or make up a ' garden ' of this type you should remember that saintpaulias require humidity, ventilation and the right temperature. If these are at fault, the plants are bound to grow irregularly.

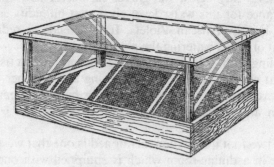

Seed tray and sheets of glass

Particularly in the United States, the basement is used for fluorescent lighting and among the advantages of such a place is that there is less likelihood of draughts because there are fewer doors. The attic cannot be recommended for not only is it usually an inconvenient place but the temperature is liable to vary tremendously being very cold in winter and hot and stuffy in the summer. As a guide for a start with fluorescent lighting, it may be a help to mention that a two-foot long tubular fluorescent lamp will provide coverage for a growing area of twenty-four inches by six inches.

CHAPTER TWENTY-FOUR

Caring for the Plants

FRESH AIR is as essential to plants, including saint-paulias, as to human beings. This is particularly so during the summer and autumn, since it is then the plants should become stronger, healthier, and strengthened to stand winter conditions. A plant which has been coddled and cosseted, will be the most likely to suffer from disease and pest attacks.

Fresh air does not mean draughts however, for no plants can stand these. Draughts are not only harmful to plants, but they are a waste of heat, whether in the greenhouse or living-room. If your plants are brought into the house and are kept on the window sill steps must be taken to move them away from glass during the winter, since very often the temperature close to the window, is considerably lower than in the room itself especially behind curtains.

Not only do the leaves require air, because they breathe, but the roots too, need air. This is something which is often overlooked. It is because this is so, that it is advisable to use silver sand or something similar in the potting compost, for this prevents the soil particles from packing down and becoming an airless waterlogged mass.

It is through the air that circulates in the soil that the essential soil bacteria develops. It is these bacteria which help to break down organic matter into the mineral salts which become available to the roots when they are dissolved in water. In this condition, they can be drawn into the plant.

It is when we know a little of what goes on inside a plant that we can provide for its needs. The most important food for a plant is carbon which is obtained from the air in the

form of carbon dioxide. This has an influence on the continued production of chlorophyll, a substance found in leaves
and which in fact, produces the green colouring.

When it is absent the leaves become pale and discoloured.
Another plant necessity is nitrogen which is required so that
the leaves and stem grow sturdy and become of good colour.
Then there is phosphoric acid, which is needed for really
good root development and it helps to prevent unwanted,
lush growth, which may occur if there is too much nitrogen.

The third vital food element is potash, which is needed to
give strength to the plant, and for the development of the
reproductive organs. In addition, there are of course, a
number of trace elements which are absorbed through the
tiny root hairs which in a healthy plant, are very active and
are made so by their search for food.

Individual root hairs last only a short while, but are
rapidly replaced by others. The thick or main roots are
needed for the support of the plants and to act as a channel
for transplanting the liquid food into the stems.

Water containing the mineral salts or food is drawn up
through the roots into the leaves, which have often been
described as the factories of the plant. It is in the foliage
that the minerals are changed into the various substances
needed for growth. Some of this material is not used at once,
but is stored in various ways, often being described as starch.

One other important plant function is the evaporation of
moisture from the stomata or pores in the leaves. These are
the breathing organs through which a plant takes in the
carbon dioxide. If plants are brought into a very hot, close
atmosphere they often evaporate or lose more moisture
than can be immediately replaced, and this leads to the
foliage becoming limp and wilting.

It also occurs when plants are exposed to hot sun. Once
they are in the cool again or when evening comes, limp
plants if healthy will often be found to have righted themselves through not losing moisture so rapidly. If therefore,
we make sure that we provide our plants with the right
living conditions, give them moisture, feeding material, fresh

air and the ability to breathe properly, we are doing very much to help them to give of their very best.

When plants become sickly it pays to consider the possible causes and almost always they can be traced back to some fault or omission in cultivation. An obviously unhealthy plant should not be fed, neither should one with dry roots. It is helpful if the plants are examined at frequent intervals so that should there be any trouble it does not get out of control.

Sometimes one is led to believe that African Violets cannot be grown without central heating or some other form of special warming apparatus. Now, it is true that these plants do require a little more understanding than many other subjects but any care needed will be amply rewarded.

In Switzerland, Denmark, Norway and Sweden, saintpaulias are grown very successfully under central heating methods. In this country, where such heating is not always available, the plants can be flowered under all kinds of heating methods. Central heating is a clean and easy way of providing warmth, but it has the drawback of making the air dry. Regular sprayings with water can assist in keeping the air from becoming dry around the plants – a harmful thing, as far as saintpaulias are concerned. Such spraying is not always easy or convenient when plants are kept in the living-room.

Fortunately, other heating methods have been divised, or found, to prevent a very dry atmosphere. The small scent sprays can be used for moistening the foliage, but a far better method is to stand the pots on little blocks of wood or on moss, placed in shallow bowls of water. This not only prevents the compost in the pot from drying out, but ensures that the air is moist around the plants. The bottom of the pot itself should not actually touch the water.

Another method is to stand the potted plant in a larger pot and to pack damp moss, peat or similar material between the two pots. This again, not only stops the compost from becoming dry but provides the needed moisture around the plants.

In the greenhouse it becomes necessary to keep the plants under whatever heating methods are being employed. This can only be by hot water pipes, electricity, gas or paraffin. With all of these, the aim must be to keep the air moist, otherwise the foliage will become discoloured and the plants gradually become unsatisfactory.

One need not be afraid of using paraffin for heating since properly employed, it is quite satisfactory. It is, of course, important to maintain a small crack of ventilation, even in cold weather. The danger of fumes certainly exists, and the difficulty here is that, although it is easily possible to detect the normal paraffin odour, fumes have no smell at all.

When the plants have passed out of their first years' flowering they should not be neglected. It is so easy to lose really fine plants because the roots have been kept too wet leading to the rotting of both the roots and the crown. Saintpaulia plants will come through the winter where the temperature does not fall lower than 50 degrees F. although rather more warmth is better.

From September onwards, growth is much slower and since the somewhat hairy foliage is liable to collect dust, the plants sometimes look a little jaded. It is therefore helpful if saintpaulias are given a really good spraying, every fourteen to twenty days, with a solution of Volck which is a white oil insecticide. Not only does it destroy insects but it keeps the foliage in good condition. It should be used at the rate of one and a half fluid ounces to each gallon of water.

In the autumn, do not be afraid to dip the plants in a Volck solution. Carefully and gently plunge them in and out of the solution, in order to assist the washing effect. If the plant is held properly there should be no danger of the soil coming out of the pot.

In February, one can usually determine which plants are ready for potting on. As always, use clean pots not forgetting that the crocks should be clean too. Water the plants a few days before they are being potted on and take off any very old or badly marked leaves. Use a good potting mixture as mentioned elsewhere and pot firmly, making sure not to bury any of the leaves. After potting stand the plants in a warm part of the greenhouse where they are not likely to be affected by draughts.

As we have already stated, the question of humidity is of great importance and is naturally, connected with the way in which the plants are watered. Where a number of plants are being grown in the greenhouse, a special piece of staging can be arranged.

Instead of having an ordinary slatted staging, a sheet of asbestos can be laid over the slats and a number of holes can be bored into the asbestos to allow the warm air to rise up around the pots, and also to provide drainage and prevent sourness through possible overwatering. On the asbestos should be placed a two-inch layer of shingle or sand. If this material is kept just moist, it will both help to prevent the roots drying out and provide a moist atmosphere giving humidity during the summer months which is just what the plants like.

This does mean of course, that the shingle or other material must be kept well watered during the summer and whenever the weather is warm. If the plants are placed on saucers or something similar, it will prevent any possibility of the roots working their way into the sand.

All methods of watering African Violets are bound to be questioned. The fact is that, although the plants can be watered from the bottom, that is by standing the pots in shallow vessels of water, so that moisture seeps up through the compost, it is quite satisfactory to water into the top of the pot. The danger of the latter method as we have stated elsewhere, is that sometimes spots of water settle on the leaves, and if bright sunshine reaches the foliage, it may very well cause a scorch mark.

If the water used has had the chill off it during cool weather, this will lessen the possibility of the foliage becoming marked. We suggest that sometimes water should be applied from the bottom of the pot and sometimes from the top. One point not to be overlooked, in regard to top watering, is that when fertilisers have been applied on the surface, an application of water on the top, helps to distribute the fertiliser easily.

When standing the pots in water, they should be left there until the soil feels really damp at the top. Do not let the pots remain in water for long periods. This could cause waterlogging and prevent the necessary aeration, which in turn would cause the roots to decay and the plants to become unhealthy.

Generally speaking, one can reckon that African Violets need watering about twice weekly during the summer months, and once weekly at other times of the year. Naturally this is not to be regarded as a hard and fast rule. In the case of individual pots, they can be placed in a bowl containing half an inch of gravel, and if water is kept in the bottom of the bowl and level with the top of the gravel, there will be slow evaporation which will benefit the plant.

To ensure continuous blooming feeds of liquid manure can be given occasionally. These take the place of ordinary water, and are very much easier to apply than solid feeds. This fertiliser does not have any unpleasant smell, which is a valid objection to some plant foods.

Although nowadays quite a lot of saintpaulias, gloxinias, and other plants, are grown successfully in the living-room, many others are cultivated in the greenhouse. It is, of course, quite a common practice to grow the plants in the greenhouse, and to bring them into the living-room where they remain as temporary plants, going back into the greenhouse after the flowers have finished.

The question of heating is one which occupies the attention of all greenhouse owners. It is not always easy to provide electricity, or an elaborate pipe-heating system. Fortunately, paraffin can be used with great success. This almost invariably takes the form of portable convectors.

The lamp burners in these heaters are usually fitted with flat wicks, which produce the well known yellow flame of burning paraffin, or they may be fitted with circular wicks, and burn vaporised paraffin, which with air, gives a blue or Bunsen flame. These blue flame burners give off more heat, and provide perfect combustion, of the paraffin, which is not always so with the yellow flame burners, but they do, of course, also need more exact adjustment and great care in maintenance.

These heaters having to be used inside the greenhouse, draw their air from the supplies inside the house, therefore, houses in which such heaters are used cannot be closed down entirely. The ventilators must always be open, to admit fresh air, and allow the products of combustion to escape. This means of course, that it is difficult to maintain a pre-arranged temperature, but when the right size of heater is used they do keep the temperature above freezing point.

The best quality paraffin must always be used and care is needed so that it is not splashed in any way. Whenever paraffin is used the question of fumes arises. The products to provide combustion of paraffin, consist of carbon dioxide and superheated water vapour, neither of which are harmful to growing plants.

Dangerous fumes are given off only if combustion is imperfect. It is not the paraffin smell which is harmful, but the fumes, which are odourless. There are several causes of the production of imperfect combustion, these include the imperfect adjusting or dirty wick, lack of proper ventilation. and poor quality paraffin.

There should certainly be no trouble if the wick is trimmed regularly and if the burner is kept scrupulously clean.

Leaves sometimes fall from plants, and this can be a very worrying occurrence. It will happen where there are great changes of temperature which give a shock to the plant, or where plants have been bought in winter and are then kept in a room where the temperature is entirely different from that in which they were previously kept. Draughts too will often cause the leaves to fall. Occasionally too leaves will become discoloured. although there are no signs of disease. It is natural for foliage to fall occasionally and if it does not continue there is nothing to worry about. Poor, weak, spindly growth which is sometimes seen is likely to be caused by lack of light and the absence of sufficient feeding matter in the soil.

Since the leaves of African Violets are of soft texture they easily mark or scald when exposed to direct, strong sunshine. While the plants should have plenty of good light, they should therefore, be kept out of hot sunshine at all times. When the sun is less powerful in the early morning or evening, they will not suffer harm. This is why a North, North-East or even an East facing window provides a good position for the plants after their flowering period, which lasts from May until September.

As with other types of plants, it will soon be noticed from the appearance of the foliage whether saintpaulias are flourishing and should the leaves indicate otherwise, the plants should be moved. When the leaves become a pale yellowish shade, it is almost certain they have become affected by sunshine, while very dark green leaves with few flowers, indicates the plants requiring more light.

A suitable temperature in which to keep the plants is around 60 degrees F. although the plants will actually grow well when it falls as low as 50 degrees or rises to 75 degrees or so. As with all plants, when the temperature is low, the soil must be kept on the dry side. The general culture required for African Violets can be summed up under the following headings: light, temperature, moisture and sufficient feeding matter in the soil.

Slight air humidity keeps the plants in good order and if the only place where they can be kept is one on the south side of the house, shade must always be provided during sunny periods. For good, regular growth, watering is important but never apply moisture unless the plants need it. Many growers keep their plants on a gravel base which is kept moist but in such cases, the base of the pots must not come into actual contact with the gravel. Therefore, the aim should be to stand the plants over, but not in water. If applying moisture directly into the pot use lukewarm water, for very cold water is liable to give a check.

The saintpaulia is really no more difficult to grow than many other subjects which are now regarded as 'house plants'. For those who wish to start a collection right away it is, of course, better to purchase mature plants. This however, is not always the best method. If plants in bloom are bought, they may very well resent the change from the greenhouse or similar conditions in which they have probably been raised and the flowers may soon fall.

This will result in a lapse of time before the next flush of flowers appear which will be when the plants have settled down in their new positions. African Violets produce only one flower bud from each leaf axil so that when one flower falls prematurely, it is usually necessary to wait for the next tier of leaves to develop before new buds form.

It is, of course, possible to raise plants from leaf cuttings which can be purchased from specialist growers. This means waiting for seven months or so before the first blooms appear. Raising plants from seed also means that there is a fairly long waiting time for colour to show. Against this, of course, there is the excitement and anticipation of wondering exactly what sort of flowers the plants raised from seed will produce. The best way to start a collection, and to have blooms in a short time, is to buy strong young plants just showing signs of developing flower buds. Such specimens will easily be able to settle down under the conditions available, and there should not then be any question of bud drop or the plants becoming weak because of the change of surroundings.

CHAPTER TWENTY-FIVE

Some Good Varieties

WHICH ARE the best varieties of saintpaulias, is a question which is often asked. It would be difficult, in fact, impossible to truthfully answer such a poser. There are many hundreds of good varieties in cultivation, but one cannot help wondering what has happened to some of those which were introduced only a few years ago in such glowing terms.

Then it will become obvious that many varieties, although good, do not become really commercial sorts, and gradually fade out of the catalogues. Many of these will continue to be found in amateur collections long after the professional grower has discarded them for lack of demand. Some, of course, disappear because they are poor doers and hardly worth the extra trouble needed to grow them well. Others readily succumb to crown rot, or have some other disorder.

Gradually it becomes a matter of the survival of the fittest, and as far as catalogues are concerned, those for which there is demand. Sometimes, of course, the really keen commercial grower continues to cultivate and offer sorts which he knows to be good, and which he likes, even if there is little demand for them.

The African Violet lover will certainly want to grow some of the rather more difficult kinds. These act as a challenge which if accepted, usually brings fine rewards. The question of names is important, and undoubtedly sometimes has an effect on the popularity of the variety. One should not be too persuaded by some of the funnier names used nowadays. Some titles which may be found in Amercian catalogues are easy to remember, although so often they have a significance only to those who know the origin or area in which they were once raised.

Any list of varieties is bound to become dated after a few years, but the following varieties are good, and take in a wide colour range. Grown under good conditions they will prove very rewarding and it is hoped that the selection detailed will give an insight to the remarkable number of varieties in cultivation, although we still await with eagerness the introduction of a yellow variety.

Africa. A fringed dark purple, with a tendency to a chartreuse edge on the lower petal. The very dark foliage is fringed and ruffled with a dark red reverse. A vigorous easy to grow plant.

Afterglow. Long lasting double cerise pink flowers, on attractive girl type foliage. Almost perpetual blooming.

Amethyst. A pale mauve single, is an old favourite.

Assynt. A seedling of Ionantha. Single rich blue flowers on very strong medium green foliage.

Big Blue. Extra large, double, mid-blue flowers carried in large clusters on strong stems held above pale green, boy type foliage.

Big Boy Blue. This has semi-double, large, intense blue flowers on vigorous boy type foliage.

Black Magic. Still one of the best of the dark double blues. Very free flowering. Blooms enhanced by a cluster of bright yellow anthers.

Blue Boy. Although now an old variety, this is still one of the most popular of the single deep blues.

Blue Cluster. Large bright blue, dark green foliage with red underside. Effective in a hanging type of container.

Blue Lady. Sky blue. A good companion to Blue Boy.

Blue Nocturne. This has exquisite, light blue frilled double flowers. Medium green, waved foliage, making a most attractive plant.

Blue Pacific. Large deep blue flowers on round dark green foliage.

Calumet Beacon. Flowers semi-double lavender blue,

with diffused white edging. An attractive plant with pale green foliage.

Colonial Pink. Large medium pink flowers, with a deeper pink eye. Dark glossy green foliage and free flowering.

Dark Delight. Intense deep blue, fully double flowers. Free flowering.

Delectable. One of the best double light blues. Very free flowering on sturdy mid-green, boy type foliage.

Desdemona. (improved). Rich deep mauve-red single blooms, freely carried above compact foliage. One of the best.

Dixie Moonbeam. Unusual blue network pattern on white.

Double Dandy. Very large round dark blue flowers, on dark green foliage.

Double Orchid Prince. Large very double, red orchid flowers on fresh green quilted foliage.

Double Red Comet. Large flowered good wine-red double with strong dark green leaves.

Diplomat. Improved double deep blue Geneva flowers. Produced in perfection on strong stem, above boy type foliage.

Festivity (Wicks). A deep double blue sport from that popular variety Calument Beacon, has all its parents' good qualities.

Flamingo. A deep double pink, with some blue in it.

Flying Dutchman. Attractive deep violet single flowers, on cedar green, red backed foliage. Makes a splendid single crown plant.

Frilly Fluff. Very full, red-purple double flowers. Petals ruffled and curled forward, so lighter reverse colour shows in a two toned effect. Slightly quilted, bronze wavy foliage which is red underneath.

Fringed Snow Prince. An improvement on Snow Prince. Pure white fringed blooms set well above pale green, serrated leaves.

Fused Pink. A most unusual shade of pink. The flowers

have a rayed appearance. A very pretty plant with bright green leaves, which buds up extremely well.

Geneva Wonder. Large single, dark purple blooms, with a scintillating white edge. Vigorous round, boy type foliage.

Glowing. Large semi-double medium red flowers. Mid-green boy shaped leaves.

Independence. A semi-double red, the dark green foliage being red underneath.

Lacy Lavender. Attractive semi-double lavender flowers on dark green foliage.

Lambley Boy (Wicks). The single deep pink flowers of this variety, are enhanced by the large very dark green foliage. Free flowering, making a most shapely plant.

Lilac Time. (Wicks). Bright mauve-pink blooms on light green boy type foliage. Free flowering.

Lilian Jarrett. A hybrid with peach-pink, double flowers. Beautiful heart-shaped leaves, sometimes slightly mottled.

Loretto. An exquisite double pink lavender, with very dark glossy foliage.

Malta. A fine double blue variety of good habit. Makes a large plant, with dark green, boy type foliage.

Mayfair. Large frilled, very full, double dark purple flowers, on very dark foliage. An outstanding plant.

Mojave. Single dark mauve flowers, with white edging, held well above wavy, dark green foliage.

Pink Cloud. A good double pink, and a frequent prize winner.

Pink Cushion. Rich double pink flowers on deep green foliage.

Pink Fog. Heavily fringed, deep pink single flowers, the deep green leaves having a red reverse.

Pink Geneva. Large pink blooms, with an upturned edge of paler pink, held well above attractive pale green, boy foliage.

Pink Miracle. A lovely frilled pink, the single blooms having a deeper centre zone, and edge to petals. Deep green foliage.

Pink Polka. A lovely bright pink. Large double, round blooms, with leaves to match.

Pink Wonder. Perfect shaped, satin rose, single flowers, held erect on palish green, rounded leaves.

Pink Sensation. Slightly deeper pink than Pink Cloud. Of good flowering habit, the blooms being held well above the foliage.

Purple Frills. As its name implies, this variety has rich purple, frilled, double blooms held above dark green, red backed, boy type foliage.

San Mateo. Another near red single, with good sized blooms. Dark green, red backed foliage.

Sarnia. An excellent double deep blue. Mid-green boy type foliage.

Sea Sprite. A double fringed white, bordered with purple. Fresh green wavy foliage.

Showman. Most impressive, with white flowers often two inches across.

Silver Slipper. Beautiful clear red, cup shaped flowers, on lovely spooned girl type foliage, with silvery reverse.

Skyway. Single, large flowered, non-fading sky blue.

Snow Ballet. Double white, with few to equal this variety for size of bloom, and the vigour of its growth.

Snow Prince, A very good, single white variety, which has long been popular.

Snow Squall. An outstanding, free flowering variety. The many large clusters of single white blooms are enhanced by the pale green, slightly ruffled foliage.

Sonnet. Dark double pink, on quilted notched edge foliage.

Vanity (Wicks). A first-class double mauve reminiscent of Parma Violets. Flowers carried profusely, above well shaped, dark green boy type foliage.

Wayzata. Clusters of mid-blue flowers are carried well above the dark green quilted foliage. A vigorous and free flowering variety.

Wedding Ring. A new type double Geneva. Dark purple flowers with distinct white edges. Pale green, slightly ruffled **foliage.**

White Madonna. Free flowering, lovely girl type foliage, long lasting double white blooms.

White edged varieties: Azure Beauty, is a very attractive blue double, with irregular white markings, not a clear edge. Eclipse (Fischers), is a slightly frilled mauve with white edge. Lady Geneva which is otherwise rather like Blue Boy. Silver Lining is a beautiful double blue with white edges, and Snowline is similar, but mauve and white.

Each year sees the introduction of new varieties. Some of these do not remain in favour for long and some of course, are similar to those already in cultivation.

The following however, are all recent introductions; all are first-class. They are not given in any order of merit, but are simply listed as first-class sorts, well worth growing.

Bilko, one of the best double blues. Very large, deep blue double flowers in profusion, carried above vigorous boy type foliage.

Crown of Red. An exquisite semi-double near red. Flowers held well above boy type foliage. A most attractive plant.

Double Pink Geneva. A double counterpart of the most popular pink Geneva. Large double pink flowers, edged white.

Fairy Skies. Very large, deep blue single flowers, with scintillating white edge, strong dark green, boy type foliage.

Paul Bunyun. You must not miss this exceedingly free flowering near red double. The flowers are in large clusters and are backed with large round boy type foliage.

Persian Blue. This variety is an improvement on the old Blue Nocturne. Its light blue double flowers set well above pale green foliage, make a most attractive combination.

Plum Tip. Pale mauve single flowers, each flower petal being tipped purple. A beautiful, novel introduction.

Sir Francis. A new deep blue single. Flowers carried profusely above vigorous well shaped, dark green boy type foliage.

Violet-n-Gold. An unusual colour in African Violet blooms. Violet shaded, single flowers, with frilled edges tipped creamy-gold.

White Perfection. Vigorous in growth, with large clusters of creamy-white double blossoms, having yellow anthers. Has strong, green boy type foliage.

CHAPTER TWENTY-SIX

Propagation

CHIEFLY BECAUSE of the introduction of many good named varieties, one may be inclined to overlook the fact that saintpaulias can be raised from seed quickly and readily. One can understand that the regular introduction of new varieties of named African Violets, which have to be propagated vegetatively, has led to a decline of the growing of the species Saintpaulia ionantha.

This species however, is quite a lovely little plant which can be raised from seed without difficulty. The beautiful dark violet-blue flowers have showy, contrasting golden anthers in the centre.

Excepting in the case of S. ionantha grandiflora, which is the type of plant producing violet-blue flowers, and a few others, it is not possible to raise named varieties of saintpaulias from seed, since they do not come true to type.

Most of the leading seedsmen now supply seeds of the ionantha mixed hybrids, which produce plants having flowers in many bright colours. While the seeds need treating with care, any little extra attention that it is possible to give will be amply repaid.

The best time to sow is in the early spring, in a germinating temperature of 65 to 70 degrees F. using pans, pots, or trays of good compost. The John Innes seed compost is suitable, or a mixture of equal parts of good loam, leaf mould, peat and silver sand, can be made up without difficulty. Where just a little is needed for a small quantity of seeds, a mixture can be made up on the following lines. Two parts of loam, one part each of peat or leaf mould, silver sand or vermiculite, and old, well rotted manure. Failing the latter material, some good compost is suitable. If you are fortunate enough to obtain soil from molehills, this will prove first-class. It is important to thoroughly mix all these ingredients.

The seed is very tiny, and should be sprinkled very thinly on the surface of the soil, and be barely covered with fine silver sand. Then place a sheet of glass over the receptacles and shade from the sun and strong light by covering this with a sheet of paper, which should remain in position until growth is seen.

If the compost is nicely moist at sowing time, as it should be, little watering will be necessary until germination occurs.

If it is needed, it is best done by standing the receptacles in shallow vessels of water which should be allowed to seep up through the compost. While the seedlings should have plenty of light, they must be kept out of direct sunlight. A fairly humid atmosphere will greatly assist growth, and aid the formation of a good root system.

Germination is often fairly slow, and may be erratic, some seeds germinating well before others. With ordinary good care however, a high percentage of seeds will grow satis-factorily. If a propagating frame is available with bottom heat, so much the better.

It is possible to buy an electrical unit and a small trans-former which can be fixed to an electric plug. Heat can then be switched on and off in the usual way, and as necessary. The wiring should be covered by an inch or so of sand, and five or six inches of moist peat, into which the sown pans can be plunged.

Keep the plants out of draughts, and avoid letting the surface dry out at any time. While saintpaulias will thrive under central heating conditions it is important to keep the air moist. Fortunately where central heating is not available, they will grow in the warmth of an ordinary living-room.

Saintpaulias usually produce a number of little rosettes of leaves from the leaf axils. These are known as side crowns, and if they are allowed to develop to any great size, they will cause the parent plant to become mis-shapen. In addition, if a number of side shoots develop, they will soon take a

great deal of strength from the parent plant, thus affecting
the quality and quantity of its flowers. Therefore, such side
crowns should be removed as soon as noticed and this can
be done by simply nipping them out. Some gardeners use a
pair of tweezers for this purpose. Care is needed however in
making sure that flower buds are not removed in mistake for
side crowns, for of course, these buds are also produced from
the leaf axils.

When deciding to propagate from side crowns the base is
trimmed off clean. It is helpful if the cut portion is dusted
with green sulphur. The offsets can then be planted in two-
inch pots or pans of sandy compost. Since many of these
side crowns will have little stalk it is important to make
sure that the base of the crowns is in close contact with the
compost. A simple way of ensuring this is to peg down the
crown with a hair pin, or similar piece of metal. The compost must be kept damp, in order to encourage the roots to
develop quickly. Excepting in the case of the actual suckers,
the raising of saintpaulias from side crowns is probably
the quickest method of securing flowering plants.

After about eight weeks, young plantlets should be developing nicely, and when growth is about half an inch or
more high, they can be separated from the leaf and potted
separately. This needs to be done carefully so that the plantlets are not damaged in any way. The simplest method is to
turn the pan upside down, and gently tap the edge on the
bench or similar firm surface, so that the compost comes out
complete with rooted leaf and young plantlets still intact.
The plant should be supported between the fingers and as
much of the compost as possible, carefully removed. Then
the parent leaf should be held firmly in the soil and if carefully, but sharply pulled the rooted plantlet will come away
easily. They usually need separating from each other since
they form close together. Where stock is short the same
parent leaf can be replanted with its roots intact and thus
re-set, it will produce a further crop of plantlets. They should
then be potted up singly using a good soil mixture as previously recommended. As the late autumn approaches, they

are best kept in a propagating frame until they have become really established.

Sometimes it is found that a fairly old but good plant is available which one wishes to retain but the leaves are untidy. Such a plant can be rejuvenated by cutting through the main stem below the lowest leaves. Then place this top part firmly in a pan or pot of good compost. Usually roots will form quickly forming a strong, healthy plant which will go on growing happily for a long time.

Another fairly simple means of vegetative propagation is by striking leaf cuttings. For this, select mature leaves, which are neither old nor very young. Those from the middle tier of leaves are usually suitable. Carefully remove them with a sharp knife, and trim so that there is about an inch of stalk left.

The method of trimming the base of the cutting is open to question. Some growers find it best to make an ordinary square cut as is used for other types of leaf cuttings. Other growers say that a chisel-shaped end produces more plantlets. A third group of raisers have found if the end of the stalk is given a notched cut, about three-sixteenths of an inch long, to divide the end of the stalk into two halves, that this is the best way of ensuring good reproduction. Experience shows however, that all three methods can be used successfully, with little difference in the final results.

If the trimmed cutting is allowed to dry off for an hour or so before insertion in the compost, this seems to lead to quicker rooting. Not all growers do this. Some put in the cuttings as soon as they are prepared. Bury the end of the stalk about a quarter inch deep, making sure it is in close contact with the compost. It is helpful if the leaf is supported in some way, an ordinary plant label being quite suitable.

To conserve moisture, it is an advantage if the planted cuttings are placed in a glass frame, or an upturned jam jar can be placed over each pot containing a leaf cutting. This prevents the compost drying out, always an undesirable happening.

If a number of cuttings are being rooted, they can be

inserted in the ordinary seed tray and sheets of glass can be placed each side, with one on top, so as to produce a propagating case. After being planted and covered, stand the cuttings in a warm place, where they are out of full sunlight. Leaf cuttings can be taken at any time of the year, but during the colder periods, a propagating case with bottom heat must be considered a necessity.

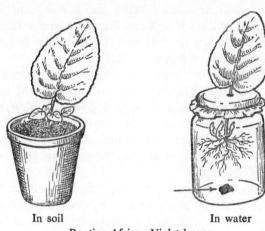

In soil   In water
Rooting African Violet leaves

There are various mediums which can be used for rooting leaf cuttings. These include the following: fine peat; coarse silver sand; horticultural grade vermiculite, which is now sold under a number of trade names; a mixture of sand and vermiculite; a mixture of peat and sand, and sphagnum moss which has been grated and sieved so that it is really fine.

Sphagnum moss and peat can also be employed. Most growers however, like to use a mixture consisting of two parts of good loam, and one part each of fine peat and silver sand. Excepting in the case of the latter, there is little or no feeding value in any of the other mediums, so that it is important for the rooted cuttings to be moved whilst they are still small.

After a period of seven to nine weeks, young plantlets will be seen developing at the base of the parent leaf. They should be carefully separated and potted up separately on the lines suggested for rooted side crowns on page 155. They should then go on to form a good root system, and build up really strong plants.

Saintpaulia plants raised from leaf cuttings early in the year will give a good show of bloom from the end of the summer onwards. In the following year it is a good plan to select the best of such plants and put them in five-inch pans of good compost. There, they will make a really large plant giving a fine display of flowers.

As soon as the first year plants have finished their main flowering season in the autumn, watering should be continued with care. It is easy to spoil plants by keeping the roots too wet. This leads to the rotting of the roots and crown. If not kept too wet the plants will over-winter quite well in the greenhouse, so long as the temperature does not fall below 50 degrees F.

As the autumn advances, the fresh foliage will be slower to develop, and the somewhat hairy leaves are liable to collect dust and dirt. When this happens, the finest looking plants will eventually become of a jaded appearance. This condition can easily be prevented by spraying the plants every two or three weeks, with a solution of Volck, which is a white oil insecticide. It is sufficient to add one and a half fluid ounces to each gallon of water used.

When the leaves are dirty, they can be dipped in this solution, and gently moved up and down in order to get rid of the dirt. To prevent the accident of the plant falling into the solution, the first two fingers of the left hand should be placed on top of the ball of soil, one finger each side of the plant. The pot can then be turned upside down with the other hand, and the plant can be dipped into the solution and washed without the soil being made wet at all.

Not only will such washings encourage a healthy, vigorous appearance, but it will keep the plant free from insects and pests, and lessen the possibility of disease. By the following early spring, it should be possible to decide which plants are going to be potted on. Here again, it is best to keep only the finest specimens and to depend upon young stock for replacements.

Always use clean pots and clean crocks for the bottom of the pots. The compost used can be a simple mixture made up of peat, loam, sand and a good base fertiliser which in fact, is a mixture in which saintpaulias usually flourish. Make sure the plants are watered a day or so before re-potting and when doing this job, remove discoloured, bruised or broken foliage. Pot fairly firmly, making sure that the compost is brought into close contact with the old ball of soil.

Since saintpaulia leaves are hairy, care is needed so that they are kept clean. Once potting on has been completed, the plants should be kept on the greenhouse staging in the warm, where they will be out of draughts. Protection from strong sunshine is always needed.

If you happen to have a propagating case into which the plants can be placed, this will be first-class, more especially so if bottom heat is available. After the plants have been in the case for three weeks or so, more air can be admitted with some slight damping to the inside of the glass.

Polythene bags have long been used for the preservation of plants. Some years ago as a result of trials by the Royal Horticultural Society, saintpaulia leaf cuttings were successfully rooted in sealed polythene bags. They were retained there until they were nicely rooted and ready for transferring into two-inch pots.

They were in the bags for not less than fourteen weeks, and during that time, the bags were not opened and the leaves did not require any attention at all. The bags used were made from three-inch wide material cut to seven-inch lengths. About a three-quarter inch depth of soil was put into each bag and thoroughly moistened. The prepared leaf cuttings were then inserted about a quarter inch deep, the top of the bag being sealed by clamping it between two metal strips.

The bags were placed against a wall at the back on a

shelf although some were hung on a line with small clips. It was found best to use square ended bags, for this allows more room for the young plantlets. It was found that by folding the tops twice over a narrow strip of plant label and fixing them with a clip the bags were satisfactorily sealed.

The result proved to be very good, for apart from a few older leaves, which may have been damaged before insertion and therefore bruised, rooting was very even. Treated in this way it was found that leaves inserted in August or September had made nice plants within six weeks or so. After this time, another couple of weeks was needed before the plants developed. Once it was decided to take the young plants from the bag separation was quite easy.

The experiments were carried out with various mediums including ordinary soil and sand. As a further experiment the ends of some stalks were kept held just above water level in the bag. In each case, rooting was very even but with the water method, the plants needed to be potted as soon as roots and plantlets appeared to be developing.

Although moisture normally condenses on the inside of the bag and may also come into contact with the leaf, the experiments showed, almost surprisingly, that no real damage from damping off occurred. It is thought that it is not only moisture itself which leads to damping off but the cooling by evaporation, which is also likely the cause of discoloration and decay.

A very simple way of increasing stock where no special facilities are available for propagation, is one which can be practised by almost anyone. First secure a one pound jam jar or a similar glass vessel and fill it to the brim with water. If at all possible use rain water. Then tie paper over the top just as is done when jam is made. Make three or four holes in the paper without tearing it, and insert a good selected leaf into each hole, making sure that the stems are poked down well, and so that the leaf blade is only just clear of the paper.

Too many cuttings in a jar will lead to tangled roots

35. A carpet of Begonia Blooms exhibited at the Anglo-Belgium exhibition.

36. A Mechanically Operated Butterfly at the London Anglo-Belgium exhibition.

37. *Right*: Another fine Specimen
Ruffled Flower.

38. *Below*: A Modern Ruffled Form.

which will easily be damaged when the cuttings are removed. Top up with water if necessary, making sure that the water used is at the same temperature as that already in the jar. Then stand the jar in a window or a similar place where there is plenty of light, but out of reach of direct sun.

Within six or seven weeks the typical white roots will be noticed pushing out from the bottom of the stem. A little later very small leaves will be seen showing at the base of the leaf blade. As soon as the largest of these new leaves is about half an inch high, the leaf cuttings are ready for potting up separately. For this, use a good fairly rich, well drained compost, such as previously recommended. Three-inch pots which should be well crocked, are very suitable, for this purpose.

The moving operation requires great care since the tiny young roots are very brittle and it is also easy to break or damage the little leaves. Some growers find it best to cut off the old leaf blade after the rooted cuttings have been potted. This should not be done for a week or so after removing the cuttings from the jar since the old leaf is of use in helping the cuttings to make roots in the compost. Then of course, there is the additional shock given to the young specimens if the old leaf is removed at the same time as potting up is done.

F

CHAPTER TWENTY-SEVEN

Exhibiting African Violets

THE SAINTPAULIA is an excellent plant for exhibition purposes. The range of coloured hybrids now available enables both individual plants and groups to be staged. As far as quality is concerned, judges give special consideration to condition and quality. The plants should be fresh looking and free from weather damage, pests, diseases and bruising. A collection of varieties should be staged in such a way as to display the plants to best advantage.

The leaves should be free of dust, and not marked either by ring spots or sun scorch. The container too, should be really clean. So often one sees good plants exhibited, but the pot or other container spoils the appearance.

Attention must be given to the schedule details, since at some shows it is permissible to exhibit saintpaulias with the pots showing. At others the pots have to be covered, either by being concealed in sphagnum moss, or by being planted in ornamental baskets. Generally speaking, ribbons and other attachments should be avoided.

The aim should be to exhibit a single crown plant with no side shoots at all. The plants should be showing plenty of flowers although since some varieties are more floriferous than others, it will not be possible for all plants to be showing the same number of flowers and a competent judge will know this. He will give proper consideration to the fact that some varieties are more difficult to get into bloom than others. Therefore, a really good flowering specimen of a difficult variety will be preferred to a bigger specimen of an easier to grow sort.

When removing any faded flowers make sure to take

162

away the stalk as well, so as not to leave stubs. Care is needed in this operation so that the later buds or the foliage are not bruised in any way.

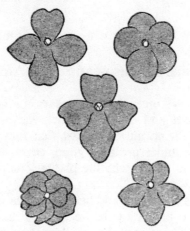

Double Flower
Showing different shapes of African Violet flowers

The serious exhibitor will commence show preparations very early, in fact, will begin to train the plant from its earliest stages. This will encourage the leaves to develop symmetrically around the plants. This even development can be encouraged by gently moving irregularly placed leaves, and fixing them in position with a tiny support. If done gradually, there should be no fear of breakages, and they will eventually grow in the desired position and the support can be removed.

Labelling is important at shows. Although, unless the schedule clearly stipulates plants must be named, the absence of a label will not disqualify the plant, if judging is tight, the labelled plant will certainly come in front.

Never leave show plants exposed to draughts even for a few minutes, and remember that plants subjected to low temperatures will soon drop their flowers. Take special care when removing saintpaulias from the containers in which they are brought to the show so that the foliage is not damaged in any way.

CHAPTER TWENTY-EIGHT

Pests, Diseases and Disorders

ALTHOUGH I think it is necessary to include details of pests, diseases and disorders which may possibly affect saintpaulias, it by no means follows that they are bound to appear. Grown under ordinary good, clean, healthy conditions, there is no reason why the plants should be adversely affected in any way.

Even so, it is advisable, and helpful, to know of the possibilities so that they may be recognised and dealt with immediately they are seen. In this way they can be stopped before they gain a real hold. While the plants of one's own raising can be watched and cared for, from their earliest stages, sometimes one has to buy from florists or open markets. There, they may have become affected by some trouble from other plants.

There are a number of specialist growers in this country whose stocks are first-class in every way, and may be thoroughly relied upon. Then, of course, one often has to grow saintpaulias in a greenhouse containing a variety of plants so that while they may not normally be liable to particular troubles, they may pick them up from other unhealthy subjects.

It is always a good plan to cast a critical eye over the plants at frequent intervals and this especially applies to specimens which have been bought or received as a present. It is perhaps advisable to keep any imported African Violets away from one's older stock for a few weeks, to ensure that the new plant is not unhealthy in any way.

Should it ever be noticed that a plant is of unusual appearance, it is best to keep it separate until the trouble can be determined. So often the foliage becomes limp giving the appearance of some disease whereas all that is needed is a thorough soaking, in fact, one should always make sure that the roots do not lack moisture before applying any insecticides or other treatment to an unhealthy looking plant.

An unhealthy plant is much more likely to succumb to disease or pest attacks than one which is growing well. It is always advisable to use clean water, and helpful if the pots are free from rubbish and scum of all kinds. Many growers insist on using sterilised soil, but this is not really essential, since a good potting mixture as suggested earlier, will normally bring good results.

As far as pests are concerned, Cyclamen Mite is liable to harm the plants seriously. Unfortunately, it is very tiny and cannot usually be seen without the aid of a magnifying glass. They vary in colour from dirty white to light brown. There are several types, some confirming their attention to particular plants. The one which attacks saintpaulias, lives on the lower leaf surfaces, sucking the juice from these, causing the leaves to curl, become brittle, and to assume a deep purplish colour. The flower buds also wither often dropping off, and those which do open, remain small and distorted.

As with all pests, prevention is better than cure, and therefore the plants should be very carefully examined at frequent intervals. There are several remedies, some of them a little dangerous to use. Perhaps the simplest way of dealing with the pests is to dust the plants frequently with Flowers of Sulphur, making sure to reach the undersides of the leaves.

This treatment should be carried out about seven times, at four-day intervals, after which the plants can be given a spraying of water which has the chill off, in order to remove all traces of powder and the possibility of staining.

Mealy Bug, of which the proper name is Pseudococcus, are very small creatures which cover themselves with a white or greyish-white cottony or waxy substance. They often seem to settle along the veins on the undersides of the leaves and growth is weakened. Mealy Bugs move slowly, and suck the sap from both leaves and stem, and if not checked will entirely spoil the plant. If the pests are noticed they should be dabbed with cotton wool which has been dipped in alcohol.

The plants need to be examined every few days, after an attack is seen, so that any hatching eggs can also be destroyed. After the plants have been treated, the foliage should be carefully dipped in slightly warm water to prevent any possibility of the leaves being damaged in any way by the alcohol. Other methods of getting rid of Mealy Bug, include the sponging of the leaves with Liquid Derris or the spraying of the plants with pyrethum or petroleum oil emulsion.

Red spider is only likely to occur where plants are kept in dry air conditions which includes central heating. They can do much damage by sucking the sap from the leaves, which then become grey and thin, before turning brittle. These pests are very tiny, but can be easily seen under a magnifying glass. They are unlikely to appear when the plants are kept under healthy conditions and the atmosphere does not become extremely dry.

Sometimes they are introduced when the plants are purchased, and they can even be brought in from cut blooms. This is why it is always advisable when buying new plants, not to place them immediately among other specimens you may have. Give the plants a little while to settle down, to show whether they have any unusual characteristics. Red spider cannot stand moisture so that regular overhead sprayings of water, especially if a Derris solution is sometimes used, will help to get rid of them.

Springtails, sometimes known as Ground Fleas, look like tiny white worms which usually work on the surface of the soil. They come where there is decaying vegetable matter in the soil, and where it is wet. They do not appear to do any harm, but their presence is unwanted. Horticultural pepper dust has been found to get rid of them.

Nematodes are other very tiny soil insects. Their presence is usually detected when the plant is taken out of the pot, and the roots are found to have little lumps on them. If the attack is not severe, the affected roots can be moved but since there is no real cure, any specimens which are badly affected are best destroyed.

Scale insects are sometimes a trouble, and since they have the ability of attaching themselves so that they look like part of the plant, they are not always easy to discover. These pests suck the sap from the leaves and stem, causing paleness and the attacked parts eventually become pitted where the insects have been working. Fortunately, once they have been found they can be destroyed, since they rarely move. While it is easy to detect them on fairly thick leaved plants, quite a useful method is to prick them off with a needle or pin. To help the plant, once the pests have been removed, spray with a good mild insecticide.

Thrips are common pests of the greenhouse, attacking many types of plants. They vary in colour some being black, others yellowish or brown. The eggs are laid on the under surface of the leaves, and the almost transparent insects which hatch out, feed on the foliage, forming white patches or streaks often surrounded by black specks.

They breed very freely and if their presence is suspected, it is a good plan to shake the plants over a sheet of white paper where many of the thrips fall and can easily be seen and then be destroyed. There appears to be several species of these pests, one being suspected of carrying a virus. Treatment is to avoid a hot, dry atmosphere, and to carefully spray with a weak nicotine wash.

Occasionally worms find their way into pot plants, very often through the compost used or sometimes when pots are placed outdoors for short periods. To avoid the latter possibility, it is always best to stand the pots on a solid base or over perforated zinc, which will prevent entry. This applies especially when pots are buried in the garden for short periods, as is sometimes advised.

Whilst aphids or green fly need not be a major menace, they may certainly attack plants of all kinds. It is during the period from March to October that attacks are most likely, and once the pests settle on a plant, they increase very rapidly unless destroyed at once.

There are of course also black or brown flies which may infest the plants. All usually go for the centre of the plants or settle on the undersides of the leaves. The effect of such attacks causes the foliage to cockle and become discoloured, since of course sap is drawn from the leaf veins. Very often too, infested leaves become sticky and this may be followed with a black substance making the plants altogether unsightly. There are numerous remedies, but since some cannot be used without the possibility of damage to certain plants, it is best to go for the milder types and not to use them too strong. This should lessen any possibility of the leaves or flowers becoming marked.

Among the few disorders to which saintpaulias are susceptible are Ring Spot and Leaf Scorch. The first shows as a yellowish spotting on the foliage which is readily caused by the use of too cold water on the leaves or by the sun shining on the globules of water on wetted foliage. This, of course, is due to exposing the plants to too strong sunlight. While both these conditions are unsightly and will spoil the plants for exhibition purposes, they will not permanently affect the health of the plant although the remedy will be quite obvious.

As for actual diseases, the chief one is Crown rot. This is largely brought about by overwatering, especially during dull, sunless days which are not infrequent during winter. The secondary cause may very well be due to a fungus attack created by the sodden state of the soil. The central stems of the plants affected become brown and the roots disintegrate. The lower leaves become discoloured at their junction with the main stem and then wither and fall.

It is no use simply pulling off affected leaves, the main stem should be examined to see whether this is affected. If the attacked plant can be caught before it has lost all the lower leaves and even some of the upper ones it is often possible to save the plant by removing all damaged leaves. Then cut through the main stem with a sharp knife just below the healthy leaves and dust the cut with green sulphur. Do not let water come over the base of the leaves, for if it does and it remains there for any length of time, it may easily lead to decay.

Petiole or leaf stem rot is also likely to be caused by faulty watering although it has been said that the incrustation of chemical salts on the rim of the pots may cause harmful effects. Affected plants have leaf stems which become watery looking and eventually drop off. When seen, infected leaves should be picked off and the stubs dusted with Flowers of Sulphur. It is therefore helpful to examine the plants regularly to see if the petioles or leaf stalks have brown marks where they touch the pot rim. This is one of the reasons why some growers take steps to prevent the stems from touching the side of the pot by fixing material round the top edge of the pot. Other means have also been employed to ensure that the leaf stems do not contact the inside of the pot. These include the varnishing of the pot rims making sure of course, that the stems are kept off the varnish until they are dry.

As a means of preventing diseases and disorder, the pots should always be kept clean and only pure water used. Plenty of light, air and warmth will normally lead to good healthy, disease resistant growth.

Index

BEGONIAS

GLOXINIAS

AFRICAN VIOLETS